NIEUPORT 11/16 *BÉBÉ*
VS
FOKKER *EINDECKER*

Western Front 1916

JON GUTTMAN

First published in Great Britain in 2014 by Osprey Publishing
PO Box 883, Oxford, OX1 9PL, UK
PO Box 3985, New York, NY 10185-3985, USA

E-mail: info@ospreypublishing.com

A CIP catalogue record for this book is available from the British Library.

ISBN: 978 1 78200 353 3
PDF e-book ISBN: 978 1 78200 354 0
e-Pub ISBN: 978 1 78200 355 7

Edited by Tony Holmes
Cover artwork, cockpits, armament scrap views and Engaging the Enemy
artwork by Jim Laurier
Battlescene by Mark Postlethwaite

Index by Marie-Pierre Evans
Typeset in ITC Conduit and Adobe Garamond
Maps by Bounford.com
Originated by PDQ Media, Bungay, UK
Printed in China through Asia Pacific Offset Ltd.

14 15 16 17 18 10 9 8 7 6 5 4 3 2 1

Osprey Publishing is supporting the Woodland Trust, the UK's leading
woodland conservation charity, by funding the dedication of trees.

www.ospreypublishing.com

German ranks	French ranks	British ranks
Major	Commandant	Major
Rittmeister (Rittm)	Capt de Cavallerie	Cavalry Captain
Hauptmann (Hptm)	Capitaine	Army Captain
Oberleutnant (Oblt)	Lieutenant	Lieutenant
Leutnant (Ltn)	Sous-Lieutenant	Second Lieutenant
Offizierstellvertreter (OffzSt)	Adjutant	Warrant Officer
Vizefeldwebel (Vzfw)	Sergent Majeur	Sergeant Major
Feldwebel (Fw)	Sergent (Sgt)	Sergeant
Unteroffizier (Uffz)	Caporal	Corporal
Gefreiter (Gfr)	Aspirant	Private First Class
Flieger (Flgr)	Soldat	Private

Nieuport 11/16 *Bébé* cover art

On 30 April 1916 *escadrille* N3 recorded the results of the morning patrol as
follows – '(Verdun) Offensive patrol right side of Meuse river, from 10 AM to
11:30 AM by Sous-Lt [Albert] Deullin, Adjs [Louis] Bucquet and [Charles]
Houssemand. Adj Bucquet engages a Fokker without results. Sous-Lt Deullin
surprises a Fokker and fires 24 bullets at 15 metres. The Fokker dives,
smoking, then goes into a spin and crashes in the southwest border of
the forest north of Douaumont. The fall was observed and testified by
Adj Houssemand. The cowling and the windshield are splattered with
German pilot's blood.' Deullin was flying Nieuport 16 N962 when he led his
flight to aid some Caudron G 4s of C53 that were being attacked by a Fokker
E III. He quickly shot the *Eindecker* down for his third confirmed victory. Its
pilot was *Rittm Graf* Erich von Holck of FFA (A) 203, who was posthumously
credited with a Caudron destroyed, although C53 lost no aircraft. His demise
was described by an old friend, Ltn Manfred von Richthofen, then serving
with *Kampfstaffel* 8 of *Kagohl* 2, in a letter he wrote on 1 May 1916 – 'One
cannot imagine that this fine fellow doesn't exist anymore. I witnessed his last
air fight. First he shot down a Frenchman in the midst of a hostile squadron.
Then he evidently had a jam in his machine gun and wanted to return to the
air above our lines. A whole swarm of Frenchmen were on him. With a bullet
through the head, he fell from an altitude of 9000ft. A beautiful death. I am
going to fly at his funeral.' (Artwork by Jim Laurier)

Fokker *Eindecker* cover art

Formed on 23 September 1915 with Nieuport 10s, *escadrille* N68 had one
victory to its credit and had received its first Nieuport 11s when it joined the
fighting over Verdun. On 10 April 1916, however, it suffered its first casualties
when two enemy aeroplanes attacked one of its two-seaters on a long-distance
reconnaissance. Although Sgt Jean Odoul managed to bring his Nieuport 10
home, he was wounded and his observer, Capt Jean Dubois de la Villerabelle,
killed. As this artwork shows, Sous-Lt Marcel Tiberghein was similarly
unfortunate, for he failed to return from a patrol in Nieuport 11 N653
after being engaged by an Eindecker E IV. N68 subsequently discovered
that Tiberghein had been brought down and taken prisoner, credited as the
third of an eventual 12 victories claimed by Lt d R Walter Höhndorf of
Fokkerstaffel Falkenhausen. (Artwork by Jim Laurier)

Acknowledgements

Thanks to Lance Bronnenkant, Christophe Cony, Norman Franks, Bernard
Klaeylé, David Méchin, Josef Scott and Greg VanWyngarden, as well as my
longtime comrade in the study of French air arms, the late Frank W. Bailey,
for their assistance in preparing this volume. A special tip of the flying helmet
also goes to Jim Laurier for his extraordinary patience in sorting out the finer
details among *Bébé*s and *Eindecker*s in the process of illustrating the story.

CONTENTS

INTRODUCTION

If anyone in the major powers that plunged into World War I still dismissed the military value of the aeroplane in the early summer of 1914, that scepticism had been effectively quashed by the end of the year. Indeed, everyone was taking air power seriously by Christmas 1914, and the first exchanges of gunfire between opposing reconnaissance aeroplanes had broken out, from Flanders to Galicia to Tsingtao.

Inevitably, the quest for control of the skies led to experiments in aircraft specialized in that task. Given the unprecedented nature of the coming struggle, these took several forms, including machine gun-armed two-seat pusher aircraft and lumbering twin-engined multi-gun flying fortresses, before the formula ultimately fell upon swift, agile single-seat scouts armed with a machine gun fixed to fire in whichever direction the pilot pointed his aeroplane.

Since most scouts were tractor aircraft, firing a machine gun through the airscrew without shooting it to pieces posed a problem, which was met in several ways. Britain's Royal Flying Corps (RFC) avoided the dilemma entirely by relocating the engine aft, leaving the front-mounted gun with an unlimited vista at the expense of speed-bleeding drag produced by the latticework of struts and wires that were required to support the empennage while clearing the airscrew. In France, a series of Morane-Saulnier tractor monoplanes featured steel wedges attached to their propellers to deflect whatever bullets came their way. Nieuport, on the other hand, literally found a way around the problem by mounting the machine gun above the upper wing of its sesquiplane ('one-and-a-half wing') Nieuport 10.

On the other side of the lines, the Germans came to adopt a mechanical method that involved a series of cams and push rods that stopped the machine gun whenever the propeller blades were in front of it. Conceived and patented by Swiss engineer Franz Schneider, this interrupter gear was practically applied by Dutch-born Anthony Fokker to a single-seat monoplane or *Eindecker*, which entered production as the Fokker E I.

From their introduction in July 1915, the E I and its improved progeny the E II through E IV jump-started the struggle for aerial supremacy over the Western Front with a reign of terror that the Allies called the 'Fokker Scourge'. Among the Allies' responses to the challenge until they could introduce practical synchronizing mechanisms of their own was the French Nieuport 11, which entered service just before the first major land battle to be accompanied by a concurrent struggle for aerial supremacy – Verdun.

Nicknamed the *Bébé* because of its small size in relation to the Nieuport 10 from which it was derived, the sesquiplane Nieuport 11 was, though less robust than true biplanes, superior in structure and overall performance to the German monoplane. During 1916 the Nieuport 11, and its more powerful but less tractable stablemate, the Nieuport 16, battled a succession of improved *Eindeckers* until the Germans abandoned the monoplane in favour of a new generation of biplane fighters. Even then the *Bébé*'s early successes influenced the Germans to adopt sesquiplane designs of their own – most notably the Albatros D III and D V – while Nieuport also held on to the sesquiplane format longer than it should have.

A Nieuport 11 restored in the markings of France's 'father of fighter aviation', Chef d'Escadron Charles de Tricornot de Rose, hangs from the ceiling of the *Musée de l'Air et de l'Espace* at Le Bourget, north of Paris. (Jon Guttman)

Being rotary-engined aircraft with balanced rudders and no stabilizers, both the *Eindecker* and the *Bébé* had their idiosyncrasies that required a level of flying skill to master, and the few pilots who succeeded at that, and went on to accumulate multiple tallies of enemy aeroplanes destroyed, acquired a special notoriety that captured the public imagination.

The French coined the term *'as'* (ace), which soon became standardized for someone with five or more aerial victories to his credit. The Germans came to award the *Orden Pour le Mérite* to Fokker *'Kanonen'* whose tally reached eight – a standard that would be raised later as the state of the fighter art advanced and shootdowns became more frequent. In 1916, when such paladins were still rare, their exploits became grist for a new mythic cult at a time when the war on the ground had lost its glory amid a maelstrom of mud and massacre on an industrial scale.

Even as they duelled for control of the skies, however, several of these 'knights of the air' were formulating a more systematic means of utilizing the aerial weapons they possessed. Men like Albert Deullin and Oswald Boelcke drew on their new-found experience to develop tactical doctrines for the new fighters, as well as means of employing them more efficiently and in greater numbers to achieve local air superiority. By the late summer of 1916 a new generation of more advanced fighter aeroplanes was ready to take the place of the Fokker *Eindeckers* and the Nieuport *Bébés*, but they and the men who flew them will be remembered for pioneering both the weapons and the strategy and tactics for wielding them.

Nieuport 16s of N3 are lined up at Cachy prior to departing on a 'balloon-busting' patrol in June 1916. The majority of the aeroplanes have been fitted with Le Prieur rockets. Parked furthest from the camera is the first Sopwith 1A2 to be tested by N3. (DR)

CHRONOLOGY

1913
July

Swiss-born engineer Franz Schneider patents his concept of interrupter gear for a forward-firing aerial machine gun.

1914
April

Raymond Saulnier, imitating Franz Schneider, develops interrupter gear for French machine guns, although it proves impracticable for the Hotchkiss and Lewis guns predominantly used by French aircraft.

1915
18 April

Sous-Lt Roland Garros scores his third victory using steel deflectors on the propeller of his Morane-Saulnier L, then falls into German hands.

June

Fokker E Is, incorporating a variation on Schneider's interrupter gear developed by Anthony Fokker and Heinrich Lübbe, start arriving at *Feldflieger Abteilungen* (field aviation units) along the Western Front.

1 July

Ltn Kurt Wintgens claims the Fokker E I's first victory, but it is not confirmed.

1 August

Ltn Max Immelmann is credited with a BE 2c for the first official victory in a Fokker E I.

November

First Nieuport 11s arrive at 'A' Sqn, No. 1 Wing Royal Naval Air Service at St Pol-sur-Mer.

1916
11 January

In the first multiple grouping of fighters in the German *Fliegertruppe* (air service), *Kommando* Vaux, commanded by Oblt Rudolf Berthold, fields five Fokker monoplanes, operating under the direct command of 2. *Armee* headquarters.

5 January

The first ten Nieuport 11s arrive for frontline service at *escadrille* MS31.

21 February

Battle of Verdun begins.

Nieuport 11 N1497 was christened *FOX-TROT* by its pilot, 1Sgt Egide Roobaert of the Belgian 1*e Escadrille de Chasse*. One of the few Belgians to use Le Prieur rockets against German balloons – unsuccessfully in his case – Roobaert flew 157 sorties before fatally crashing a mile offshore during a test flight on 19 December 1916. (Air-Espace-Lucht-Riumtevaart, Brussels)

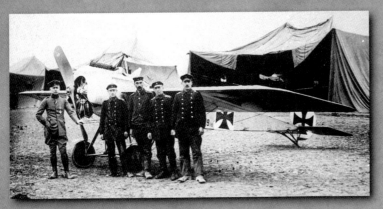

26 February	Sgt Jean Navarre downs a two-seater and a Fokker E III, raising his score to five and being declared an *as* – the first use of the term 'ace'.
10 March	Oblt Oswald Boelcke arrives at Jametz aerodrome and subsequently moves up to Sivry to establish his own frontline response unit.
15 March	Cmdt Charles de Tricornot de Rose masses fighter *escadrilles* into *groupes de chasse provisoires*.
4 May	The Nieuport 17, with wing area increased from 13 to 15 square metres and armed with a synchronized Vickers machine gun, has its first combats with *escadrille* N57
11 May	Cmdt Charles Tricornot de Rose is killed in a crash.
13 May	N124, a squadron made up of American volunteers, flies its first combat sortie from Luxeuil-les-Bains.
18 May	Cpl Kiffin Rockwell scores the first victory for '*l'Escadrille des Américains*' N124
19 May	Sous-Lt Jean Navarre of N67 becomes the first French 'double ace' with his tenth victory, but one of his closest friends, Sous-Lt Georges Boillot of N65 (two victories), is killed in action.
22 May	The French dispatch eight Nieuports to attack the German balloon line at Verdun, destroying six out of eight *Drachen* for the loss of one Nieuport 16.
24 May	Lt William Thaw of N124 is credited with a Fokker E III, but is wounded by an Aviatik in his second patrol of the day.
17 June	Sous-Lt Jean Navarre, now France's leading ace with 12 victories, is wounded in action.
28 June	Oblt Boelcke is credited with his 19th victory from the previous evening, then departs Sivry for the Balkans and Turkey – but not before writing his fighter tactics down on paper, to be distributed to German units all over the frontline.
23 July	Adj Bert Hall of N124 becomes the second, and last, member of the *Escadrille Américaine* to be credited with downing a Fokker *Eindecker*.
10 August	Oblt Hermann von der Lieth-Thomsen orders the formation of *Jagdstaffeln*, permanent fighter units ideally equipped with 14 fighters.
16 September	Five Albatros D Is and one D II are delivered to Hptm Boecke's *Jasta* 2.
25 September	Ltn Kurt Wintgens of *Jasta* 1, still flying his Fokker E IV because it mounts twin machine guns, is shot down and killed over Villers-Carbonnel by Lt Alfred Heurteaux flying a SPAD VII of N3.

DESIGN AND DEVELOPMENT

NIEUPORT 11

Founded by Edouard de Niéport in 1906, the Société Anonyme des Établissements Nieuport had already acquired a healthy reputation among aircraft builders with a series of simple, robust monoplanes when Gustave Delage signed up as its chief engineer in January 1914. His first design, the Type X, began as a two-seat monoplane to compete in the Gordon-Bennett Trophy race. When war erupted, however, the French Army declared a preference for a reconnaissance biplane, which in turn led Delage to alter his design into a compromise that he hoped would combine the best traits of biplane and monoplane.

Although designated Type XB – the 'B' referred to its biplane configuration – Delage's modified aeroplane employed a wing cellule consisting of a narrow chord, single-spar lower wing that was essentially an almost horizontal bracing strut with an airfoil section for the more conventional two-spar upper wing. The wings had a slight sweepback of 2.75 degrees, this aerodynamic feature pervading subsequent designs up to the Nieuport 28. Another trait soon to be synonymous with Nieuport products was the lack of dihedral to the upper wing, while the lower wing's dihedral could be adjusted to as much as six degrees. Delage's 'one-and-a-half wing' design came to be referred to as a sesquiplane, the shape of its interplane struts also earning his creations the English sobriquet of 'vee-strutters'.

The Nieuport XB's sesquiplane arrangement afforded the pilot and the observer a greatly improved downward view compared with that of a conventional biplane. Introduced into military service as the Nieuport 10, the two-seater came in two forms, depending on where the pilot sat – forward in the 10AV (*'avant'*) and aft in the 10AR (*'arrière'*). Powered by an 80hp Clerget or Le Rhône 9B rotary engine, the aeroplane was soon being flown by French, British, Belgian and, later, Italian aircrews.

When armament became an issue over the Western Front at the end of 1914, Nieuport installed a flexible Étevé machine gun mount in the rear observer's cockpit of the 10AV and cut a central aperture in the upper wing centre section of the 10AR, allowing the observer to stand up and fire a rifle or carbine over the propeller arc. Inevitably, a lightweight Hotchkiss or Lewis machine gun was flexibly mounted on a spigot-like device on the upper wing, affording the observer greater firepower. From there pilots began to devise fixed machine gun mounts, fairing over the observer's pit

The prototype Nieuport 10 included an upper wing mounting for a Hotchkiss machine gun, manned by the observer. This soon gave way to a fixed weapon that the pilot could fire by means of a Bowden cable to the cockpit. (Service Historique de la Défense –section'Air (SHDA))

The first Nieuport 11 prototype differed in some details from the production version, including the fitment of an inverted 'U' shaped aft cabane strut that was intended to improve the pilot's view. (Christophe Cony)

NIEUPORT 16

18ft 3.5in.

8ft 0.5in.

24ft 8in.

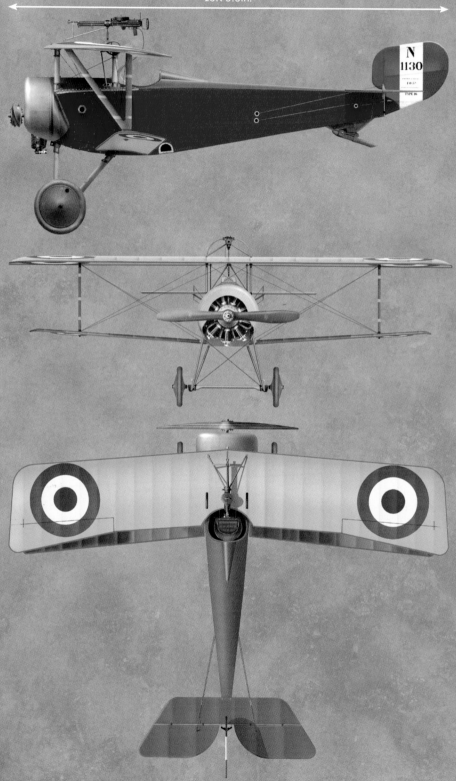

A Duks-built Nieuport 11 of the Imperial Russian Air Service has it propeller swung through prior to the engine starting. Many of the Duks-produced *Bébés* were built with pine rather than spruce frameworks, adding some 66lb of weight that had a detrimental effect on performance. (SHDA B85.2497)

entirely and duly converting the Nieuport 10AR into a single-seat fighter. A Bowden cable routed from the trigger down to the cockpit and up to a trip attached to the control column allowed the pilot to fire the weapon. As aerial hostilities intensified the French devised a variety of mountings that were hinged at the back, allowing the pilot to pull the Lewis gun down in order to reload it.

Contemporary with the Nieuport 10 was the much smaller Nieuport 11, a monoplane that was likewise given the XB's sesquiplane arrangement. Originally designated the BB-XI, and later given the military designation of 11.C1 (the suffix signifying *chasse*, or fighter, single-seat), this proportionately smaller and aesthetically pleasing progeny of the Nieuport 10 came to be popularly known as the *Bébé* (baby), a word play that sprang naturally from its first designator. It was also called the 'Type 13' in reference to its 13-square-metre wing area.

The prototype Nieuport XI first flew in the summer of 1915, and production commenced that autumn. Among the earliest recipients of the *Bébé* was the Royal Naval Air Service (RNAS), which had already made substantial orders for Nieuport 10s, and which seems to have received its first Nieuport 11 in November 1915. Since the French chose to stockpile their fighters for maximum effect, the first Nieuport 11 to reach a French frontline unit did not arrive at *escadrille* MS31 until 5 January 1916, but by February there were 90 serving in various sectors. As events would prove, they could not have come at a more critical juncture.

FOKKER *EINDECKER*

Born in the Netherlands East Indies on 6 April 1890, Anthony Herman Gerard Fokker was the son of a coffee exporter who after retirement moved back to Haarlem, in the Netherlands. After dropping out of *hochschule* and avoiding military service, Fokker moved to Germany in 1910 in an attempt to find employment in the budding aviation industry through a combination of his commercial and mechanical talents. By December of that same year an aeroplane of his own design – the *Spin* ('spider')

OPPOSITE

Jean Navarre flew several Nieuports during his time over Verdun and usually decorated them in order to be readily recognized by friend and foe alike. One had red, white and blue bands and another bore pennants in the French national colours. Nieuport 16 N1130, which was delivered in late April 1916, had a red fuselage and tailplane. Although the lower wing was in two-tone camouflage, the upper was clear-doped – it was evidently a Nieuport 11 wing used to replace the damaged original. This aeroplane was the subject of Henri Farré's famous painting showing Navarre stalking a Fokker E III. He certainly used it to bring down a two-seater in concert with Sous-Lt Georges Pelletier-Doisy of N69 on 17 June 1916, but he was seriously wounded in a subsequent combat later that same day. N1130 did not last long after this action, for it was written off at Froidos by Lt Jean Derode when he crashed on landing, demolishing the aeroplane and injuring himself.

An occasional innovator but above all else an entrepreneur, Anthony Fokker applied new concepts to practical use in order to sell aeroplanes. (Library of Congress)

Ltn d R Ernst *Ritter und Edler von Lössl* of *Feldflieger Abteilung* 21 (far left) with a Fokker M 5L (A II) – one of the unarmed scouts on which Fokker's later fighters would be based. (Jon Guttman)

– was ready for testing. By 1913 Fokker had established a factory at Schwerin and was producing *Spin* variants for civil and military use until the type was abandoned as obsolescent.

Obtaining a more up-to-date Morane-Saulnier H shoulder-winged monoplane and hiring Martin Kreuzer as his chief engineer, Fokker set out to return to the forefront of aviation's rapidly advancing state of the art. Although the M 5 single-seat *Eindecker* (monoplane) that emerged seemed to mimic the Morane-Saulnier's basic configuration, it differed from the wood-framed French aeroplane in having a structure that, aside from the wings, consisted of wire-braced chrome-molybdenum steel tubing with welded joints. Judging the Morane-Saulnier's rectangular rudder inadequate, Fokker replaced it with a comma-shaped control surface, which became a Fokker trademark for the next three years. After first powering his aeroplane with a 50hp Gnome rotary engine, Fokker modified it to use an 80hp Oberursel U 0 – a licence-built version of the seven-cylinder Gnome Lambda.

The aircraft was evaluated in two forms, namely the M 5K, whose 28.5ft (8.5m) wingspan gave it a *'kurz'* designation, and the M 5L, with a *'lang'* 31.5ft (9.6m)

wingspan and a taller dorsal pylon to support its bracing wires. The M 5L was ultimately adopted by the German *Fliegertruppe* (air service) as the A III and used in a so-called 'cavalry scout' role, gathering aerial intelligence in quick flights over the front. Lighter and easier to handle than its Morane-Saulnier counterparts, or the Pfalz monoplanes that more closely copied them, the A III became popular with pilots who flew it, including a fledgling Leutnant named Oswald Boelcke. Indeed, he wrote in December 1914 that 'The Fokker is my best Christmas present in which I take childish pleasure'.

The childish pleasures of wartime flying began to give way to a grim adolescence as competing airmen began shooting at one another with pistols, carbines, rifles, machine guns and even cannon. Then in early 1915 Sgt Roland Garros of *escadrille* MS26, who had earned pre-war fame as the first person to fly across the Mediterranean Sea, from Saint-Raphaël, in France, to Bizerte, Tunisia, on 23 September 1913, began seeking a means of firing a machine gun from a single-seat aircraft.

Raymond Saulnier had devised a mechanical, camshaft and rod-activated interrupter gear in April 1914, but had found it unworkable on open-bolt light machine guns such as the Hotchkiss and Lewis, whose inconsistent discharge rates were prone to produce hang-fires and jams. Until a better system could be worked out, Saulnier

Roland Garros in the Morane-Saulnier H in which he became the first to fly the Mediterranean, from Saint-Raphaël to Bizerte, on 23 September 1913. In April 1915 he and his armed Morane-Saulnier L terrorized the Flanders sector until he fell into German hands. (National Archives)

Photographed in August 1915, Morane-Saulnier Nm MS39? shows the forward-firing Hotchkiss machine gun and airscrew-mounted steel deflectors that allowed Garros to score three victories within three weeks. Barely workable on French aircraft, it proved impracticable for handling steel-jacketed German bullets. (SHDA B85.1192)

OPPOSITE
Fokker E II 71/16 is believed to have been flown by Oblt Hans Berr early on in his career whilst he was serving with the Fokker *Staffel* at Avillers. A Braunschweiger of French Huguenot descent, Berr served in the infantry until wounded in action on 6 September 1914. He then joined the *Luftstreitkräfte* as an observer in March 1915, later taking pilot training and being assigned to the *Kampfeinsitzer Kommando* at Avillers. His first victory – a Nieuport over Verdun on 8 March 1916 – coincided with the wounding of N69's Sgt Pierre Navarre (Jean Navarre's twin brother). This was followed by a Caudron G 4 on 14 March. When KEK Avillers was reorganized as *Jagdstaffel* 5 – by which time E II 71/16 had been wrecked in a crash landing – Berr became its first commander and raised his tally to ten on 3 November. He was awarded the *Orden Pour le Mérite* on 4 December. During an encounter with FE 2bs of No. 57 Sqn RFC near Noyelles on 6 April 1917 Berr's aeroplane collided with that of Vfw Paul Hoppe and both airmen were killed.

produced a set of steel wedges that could be bolted onto the propeller blades. Garros and his mechanic, Jules Hue, improved on Saulnier's design by narrowing the width of the propeller blades to the point where the deflectors were attached.

Installing the modified propeller and a Hotchkiss machine gun on a Morane-Saulnier L parasol, Garros temporarily joined MS23 at St Pol aerodrome, outside Dunkirk, and then went looking for trouble. On 1 April he encountered an Albatros two-seater and shot it down, killing Gfr August Spacholz and Ltn Walter Grosskopf of *Feldflieger Abteilungen* (FFA) 40. He followed that with an Aviatik on the 15th and another Albatros three days later, but soon afterwards he came down in German lines either because of engine trouble or through the severing of his fuel line by an infantryman's rifle bullet.

Ecstatic at having captured Garros and his secret weapon, the *Inspektion der Fliegertruppen* (*Idflieg*) gave the deflectors a thorough examination and ordered them adopted for German use. A problem arose, however, as the *Idflieg* soon discovered that while the wedges could deflect French copper or brass-jacketed ammunition, steel-jacketed German bullets tended to shatter them. At that point Anthony Fokker hastened to Schwerin, and within days returned to Berlin with a solution mounted on one of his M 5K *Eindeckers*.

Since 15 July 1913, Franz Schneider of the *Luftverkehrsgesellschaft* (LVG) had held a patent for using a series of cams and rods attached to the trigger bar to interrupt the machine gun's fire whenever the propeller was in its way. His idea, like the one Raymond Saulnier devised in April 1914, had been theoretical up to that time, but Fokker, spurred on by this wartime stimulus, worked up a means of putting the theories into practice. With employee Heinrich Lübbe, he devised what he called a *Gestängesteuerung*, or pushrod control, and installed it in his M 5K along with a 7.92mm Parabellum LMG 14 machine gun.

FOKKER E II

23ft 9.5in.

8ft 0.5in.

32ft 11.6in.

Although Fokker was subjected to subsequent lawsuits by Franz Schneider and August Euler over infringement of their earlier patents – and might just as well have had to face one from Raymond Saulnier if there had not been a war on – the fact remains that he took what had hitherto been a theoretical concept and put it to practical use.

Fokker's *Gestängesteuerung* consisted of hooking the trigger bar of the gun to a connecting rod running out in front of it, through an L-type rocker, to a cam follower rigidly attached behind the rotary engine. A one- or two-lobed cam attached just behind the engine's spark ring allowed the trigger bar to activate the trigger sear and fire the gun only when the propeller blades were not aligned in front of it. A trigger on the control column, connected by a Bowden cable, raised or lowered an intermediate section in or out of place to activate the process by connecting the lip of the trigger bar to the cam follower. Although this simple system caused a slight reduction in the rate-of-fire, from 600 to as low as 526 rounds per minute, it remained quite adequate for the task at hand.

After testing at Döberitz on 19–20 May, the German High Command was impressed enough to order five machine gun-equipped A IIIs and M 5Ks (designated M 5KMGs and bearing the serial numbers E 1/15 to E 5/15), followed on 28 August by a production order for 36 E Is, as the armed monoplanes were redesignated. Production E Is subsequently had their wings lowered on the fuselage, somewhat improving the pilot's downward view.

Although closed-bolt machine guns proved more amenable to Fokker's interrupter gear than the Hotchkiss and Lewis had to Saulnier's, even their suitability varied. The first armed product of Fokker's Schwerin factory, A III A16/15, was issued in July to Ltn Otto Parschau of FFA 62 at Douai aerodrome. In a letter to Fokker on 28 July, Parschau complained that its Parabellum LMG 14 incessantly jammed after a few shots, but noted that other Fokkers using the Spandau-produced Maxim LMG 08 performed excellently. Fokker quickly exchanged weapons accordingly.

The first Fokker to bear the *Eindecker* designation (E I 5/15) was issued to Ltn Kurt Wintgens, a bespectacled 20-year-old army officer's son from Neustadt who had

Ltn Otto Parschau familiarizes himself with the M 5K while Anthony Fokker poses for the camera to the right of the aeroplane. The wing had been repositioned and the troublesome Parabellum LMG 14 machine gun replaced with the Spandau-built LMG 08 by the time the fighter entered production as the Fokker E I. (Library of Congress)

received the Iron Cross 2nd Class as an observer over the Eastern Front, before undertaking flight training and then serving in FFA 67 and 6b. It was with the latter Bavarian unit that Wintgens claimed a Morane-Saulnier L east of Lunéville on 1 July 1915. Because there were no witnesses to confirm the aeroplane's demise behind French lines, the first German fighter victory remained unofficial. French records, however, noted that Capt Paul du Peuty and Lt Louis de Boutigny of MS48 had in fact force landed, both wounded. After another unconfirmed Parasol claimed on 4 July, and a transfer to FFA 48 at Mülhausen the next day, Wintgens was finally credited with a Morane-Saulnier over Schucht on the 15th – although ironically, the French recorded no casualties between 14 and 18 July!

Meanwhile, in June, two more members of FFA 62 were given the opportunity to fly the E I in combat. Both were friends, both hailed from Saxony, both harboured aggressive spirits suited for flying fighters and both saw the future of aerial warfare in the Fokker. There the commonality ended, however, for while 24-year-old Ltn d R Max Immelmann was almost a year older than Ltn Oswald Boelcke, the former was self-centred, arrogant and accused by one of his instructors of having 'a truly childish temperament'. Boelcke professed to be a loner by nature, but was more socially outgoing and mature than Immelmann. 'You can win the men's confidence if you associate with them naturally and do not try to play the high and mighty superior', Boelcke wrote, embodying a leadership style that would help make him not only commander of Germany's first elite fighter squadron, but the mentor for a generation of German fighter pilots.

Ltn Max *Ritter* von Mulzer, standing in the cockpit of a Fokker E I, readies himself for another patrol. The first successes of Max Immelmann, Oswald Boelcke and Kurt Wintgens ushered in the 'Fokker Scourge' that brought fame to several other airmen. A partner of Immelmann's in FFA 62, Mulzer had claimed ten victories and been awarded the *Orden Pour le Mérite* by the time he fatally crashed while test flying an Albatros D I on 26 September 1916. (Greg VanWyngarden)

Being the more experienced of the two, with a previous victory scored while flying two-seaters, Boelcke got to fly the new E I first, but when he fired off a long burst at a French aeroplane his gun jammed. On the morning of 1 August a bombing attack on Douai by BE 2cs of No. 2 Sqn Royal Flying Corps (RFC) spurred Immelmann to scramble skyward in Fokker E I 3/15 and bring down one of the raiders, making its pilot, Lt William Reid, a prisoner of war (PoW). Boelcke, following Immelmann up in E I 1/15, attacked a second BE 2c, only to suffer another gun jam. He finally downed what he described as an 'English Bristol biplane' on the 19th, which may in fact have been another of No. 2 Sqn's BE 2cs, whose crew force-landed in Allied lines with a severed fuel line.

From then on Boelcke and Immelmann began wreaking havoc on Allied reconnaissance aeroplanes, striking fear in RFC squadrons in particular. 'They treat my single-seater with a holy respect', Boelcke wrote. 'They bolt as quick as they can'.

TECHNICAL SPECIFICATIONS

NIEUPORT 11

Like its forebear the Nieuport 10, the 11 *Bébé* consisted primarily of a spruce framework covered in doped linen, with a metal front cowling and a horseshoe-shaped aluminium engine cowl that allowed exhaust gases and excess oil to exit downward and to the rear. According to Macchi drawings for licence production, the wings had a 3.5-degree sweepback. The single-spar lower wing with a chord of only 0.7m (27in) was braced to the two-spar upper wing, which had an average chord of 1.2m (3ft 11¼in), by two distinctive V-shaped interplane struts. The lower wing had a dihedral of up to six degrees, which could be adjusted on the ground to allow for the weight and the type of engine being fitted. The wings and undercarriage were wire-braced, with the sesquiplane wing's spar fitting into a split ring at the junction of the 'V' shaped interplane struts. Cables were secured to this anchor point to help hold the entire cellule together in flight. The tailplane was made of steel tubing and, like the wooden wing and fuselage framework, fabric covered.

The Nieuport 11's undercarriage was a simple V-shaped affair of streamlined steel tubing, with a single axle whose 1.6m (5ft 2in) track gave it adequate stability during take-off and landing. The tailskid included a steel spring that helped brake the aeroplane upon landing.

More manoeuvrable than most contemporary biplanes, but sturdier than monoplanes braced by cables from dorsal and ventral pylons, such as those made by

Nieuport 11 N1353 displays the red star insignia of *escadrille* N103 on its fuselage side, as well as a pair of French tricolours on the cowling as a personal marking. (Greg VanWyngarden)

Morane-Saulnier, Fokker and Pfalz, the Nieuport 11 boasted stunning performance for early 1916, although it could be dangerous in a lateral skid. The Nieuport's intrinsic advantages over the Fokker *Eindeckers*, which still used wing warping for lateral control, lay in the ailerons in its upper wing, activated by cranks and rods emanating from the fuselage to the upper wing, as well as its horizontal stabilizer and elevator combination. Its balanced rudder, lacking a vertical stabilizer, was just as responsive – and capricious – as the Fokker's.

The *Bébé*'s principal disadvantage lay in its armament, located above the upper wing on one of several arrangements that underwent refinement to facilitate the means of pulling the Lewis gun back and down so that the pilot could change magazines. Whatever form they took – ultimately a hinged back post with bungee cords to help return the weapon to the firing position on French Nieuports – the above-wing mountings added drag and the Lewis guns were always tricky and dangerous to reload in the face of a 90mph headwind, exacerbated by the exigencies of combat.

Aside from the matter of reloading or clearing jams, the Fokker pilot had the benefit of a machine gun sited right in front of him in a true 'point and shoot' arrangement. On the Nieuport *Bébé*, special gunsights had to be devised and carefully adjusted to accommodate a weapon that was fixed several feet above the pilot's head.

A view into the cockpit of Nieuport 11 N1205 of N65, flown by MdL Jacques Allez from 27 July to 8 August 1916, at Cachy aerodrome. Note the conveniently located sector map. (SHDA B83.1413)

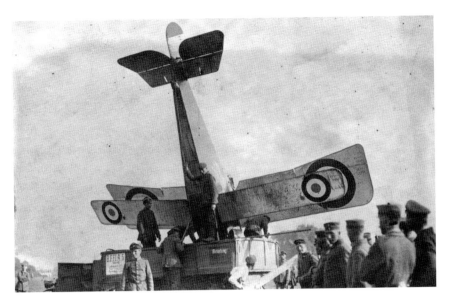

German troops load captured Nieuport 11 N1135 onto a truck, providing the photographer with a good view of its underside details in the process. Capt Jean du Plan Sieyès de Veynes, commander of N26, used N1135 to burn a balloon on 3 July 1916, only to be brought down a short while later and taken prisoner. Sieyès was released by the Germans in June 1918. (Greg VanWyngarden)

Italian Nieuport 11 Ni 2168 was built under licence by Nieuport Macchi of Varese. Tenente Francesco Baracca used a French-built *Bébé* to bring down a Brandenburg C I on 7 April 1916 for Italy's first aerial victory, and *'Niuportini'*, as the Italians called them, continued in squadron service well into 1917. Austria-Hungary's first single-seat victory, on 25 November 1915, was jointly credited to an Albatros B I crew and Hptm Mathias Bernath in a German-supplied Fokker A III (E I). The rival Nieuport and Fokker fighters seldom, if ever, met over Italy. (San Diego Air and Space Museum)

NIEUPORT 16

During the course of 1916 some *escadrilles* began installing 110hp Le Rhône 9J rotary engines in their Nieuport 11s in place of the original 80hp 9Cs – N38's mechanics, in fact, did that to all of the squadron's *Bébés*. Nieuport itself soon began manufacturing a purpose-built 110hp variant, which it designated the Nieuport 16. The airframe and dimensions were virtually unchanged from the 11, aside from a larger opening in the front of the horseshoe cowling and the addition of a faired headrest for the pilot. The similarity between the two types made it easy for the more powerful *Bébés* to supplement their 80hp stablemates over Verdun with little or no interruption in production.

NIEUPORT 11 *BÉBÉ* COCKPIT

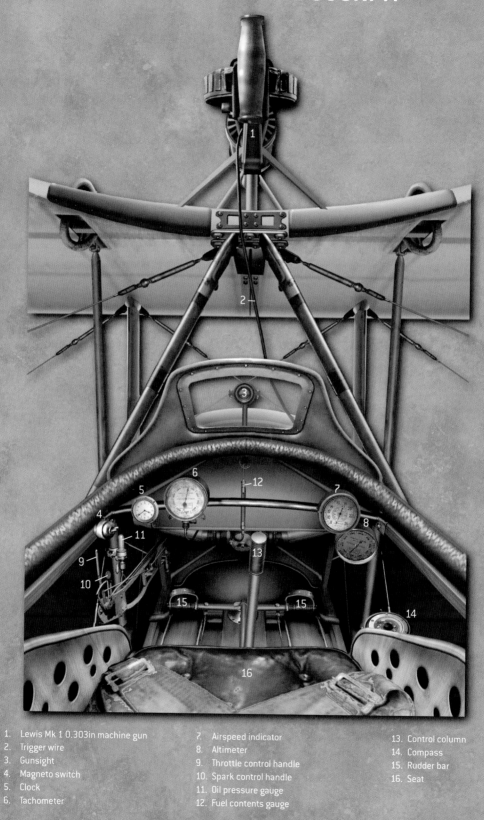

1. Lewis Mk 1 0.303in machine gun
2. Trigger wire
3. Gunsight
4. Magneto switch
5. Clock
6. Tachometer
7. Airspeed indicator
8. Altimeter
9. Throttle control handle
10. Spark control handle
11. Oil pressure gauge
12. Fuel contents gauge
13. Control column
14. Compass
15. Rudder bar
16. Seat

The more powerful engine made for a 5mph increase in speed and a considerable improvement in rate-of-climb, if comparative statistics from the Russian Duks factory are to be believed (see page 27). Pilots soon became aware of the price that came with that higher performance, however. The heavier, more powerful, Le Rhône 9J made the Nieuport 16 nose heavy and manoeuvrability was more sluggish than with the 11. Although the 16s saw a goodly amount of French use, especially over Verdun, it took an outstanding pilot to master its idiosyncrasies. This in turn meant that the type did not appear in large numbers in units assigned to less critical sectors.

One pilot who received a 16 was Sgt Jean Chaput of N31, who remarked that it was faster than anything in the sky at that time, French or German. He also stated that it could climb faster than the Nieuport 11. 'In the air it is terrific', Chaput wrote on 29 April 1916, 'but with the bad fields at our disposal in this country it is really disagreeable for landing at the moment of touchdown – it is a heavy rock thrown with the speed of a meteorite and not a flying machine'.

The Belgian Air Service obtained a solitary Nieuport 16, which was still flying in the 1ère Escadrille in July 1917 when Adj Willy Coppens joined the unit and was assigned the left-over fighter. He was probably the last pilot to fly a Nieuport 16 operationally over the Western Front. Coppens was overjoyed when Hanriot HD 1s arrived in August to replace the escadrille's Nieuport 17s, to say nothing of what he candidly remembered as his 'disagreeable little beast'.

Russia bought several Nieuport 16s and the Duks plant produced a few. The type saw only limited Russian use, however, before the Nieuport 17 replaced it. The Italians did not use the 16 at all. The only other Allied air arm to operate the type in any significant numbers was the RFC, which found its performance superior to that of the DH 2. It therefore assigned Nieuport 16s in various quantities to Nos. 1, 3, 11, 29, 60 and 64 Sqns.

Nieuport 16 N940, flown by Sgt Jean Chaput with N31 at Ancemont in April 1916, featured a front gunsight consisting of a ring suspended below the upper wing and wired to the front cabane struts. Notwithstanding its makeshift nature, Chaput used it to down a Fokker E III with only four rounds on 30 April 1916. (Christophe Cony)

At least one Nieuport 11 and several Nieuport 16s were modified with Alkan synchronization mechanisms to fire Lewis guns directly through the airscrew, but the open-bolt Lewis did not lend itself well to interrupter gear compared to the far more effective Vickers as used on the intrinsically safer and better-handling Nieuport 17.

Another innovation in armament was introduced on the Nieuport 16s escorting FE 2bs with No. 11 Sqn RFC in the summer of 1916, when a pilot in its scout detachment, Capt Herbert A. Cooper, found it difficult to change ammunition drums on the overwing Lewis gun because of his short stature. In response one of the squadron mechanics, Sgt R. G. Foster, devised a curved rail mounting that would allow the weapon to be pulled down into a vertical position in front of the pilot with much greater ease.

This 'Foster mount' became standard on British Nieuports thereafter, although another of No. 11 Sqn's pilots, Lt Albert Ball, found it an asset for another reason – it allowed him to pull down the Lewis to fire at a variety of angles in order to attack his prey from below. Ball was one of the few pilots with the skill and marksmanship to succeed at such difficult shooting, which contributed to his coming into full stride over the next few months as the RFC's deadliest fighter pilot of 1916. Another version of the Foster mount would see combat use in 1917 fitted to the Royal Aircraft Factory SE 5 and SE 5a scouts.

The obvious solution to the Nieuport 16's intrinsic handling problems was to restore its centre of gravity and overall balance with an increased wing area, and that is precisely what the manufacturer did with its 17, also known as the '15-metre Nieuport'. Incorporating numerous other refinements to the basic airframe, as well as Alkan-Hamy interrupter gear allowing the installation of a 7.7mm Vickers machine gun on the fuselage upper decking, the Nieuport 17 entered combat with N57 in May 1916, and quickly replaced the 11 and 16 alike in frontline service in the months thereafter to become the dominant French fighter until its own eventual eclipse by the SPAD VII.

The Nieuport 17's slightly enlarged airframe better accommodated the 110hp Le Rhône 9J engine than the 16's, and it was later armed with a synchronized 0.303in Vickers machine gun. N1420, however, was an early-build 17 armed with an upper wing Lewis gun. The fighter was brought down, probably by Ltn Ernst *Freiherr* von Althaus of *Kampfeinsitzer Kommando* Vaux, on 2 July 1916. MdL André Seigneurie of N103 was taken prisoner, but he escaped in April 1917. (Greg VanWyngarden)

	Nieuport 11	Nieuport 16
Dimensions		
Wingspan		
(upper)	24ft 8in	24ft 8in
(lower)	24ft 3in	24ft 3in
Wing area	143.16sq ft	143.16sq ft
Chord	5ft	5ft
Dihedral	5 degrees	5 degrees
Length	18ft 3.5in	18ft 5in
Height	8ft 0.5in	8ft 0.5in
Armament	1 x Lewis Mk 1 0.303in	1 x Lewis Mk 1 0.303in
Weight (lb)		
Empty	758	827
Loaded	1,058	1,213
Performance		
Engine	Le Rhône 9C 9-cyl 80hp	Le Rhône 9J 9-cyl 110hp
Maximum speed (mph)	97	102
Climb to 3,281ft	4 min	2.8 min
Climb to 6,562ft	10 min	6.4 min
Climb to 9,840ft	19 min	10 min
Climb to 13,123ft	33 min	16.5 min
Service Ceiling	13,123ft	15,748ft
Endurance	2.5 hours	2.5 hours

'ROCKET TORPEDOES'

In mid-1916 French fighters began to supplement their 7.7mm machine guns with a set of air-to-air rockets, also called 'rocket torpedoes', developed by naval Capt Yves Le Prieur. Fired from six to eight tubes mounted on the interplane struts, with aluminium sheathing over the fabric panels that would otherwise be flammably vulnerable to their backblast, the rockets made a spectacular show, but they were wildly inaccurate and seldom effective even at close range. Nevertheless, they were frequently mounted on the 'V' struts of Nieuport 11s and 16s engaged in the hazardous but often necessary task of venturing behind enemy lines to destroy German kite balloons, or *Drachen*, which were constantly reconnoitring French activity and directing artillery fire.

Given the rockets' tendency to shoot off everywhere except at the target, the Nieuport pilot had to dive after the 'gasbag', whose groundcrew would be using a power winch to rapidly pull it down while covering its descent with a cone of anti-aircraft artillery and small arms fire, and close to point-blank range before loosing his 'rocket torpedoes'. If the projectile did strike home, it would tear a sizeable hole in the balloon, ensuring a swift expulsion of hydrogen into the atmosphere for

Sgt Henri Réservat's Nieuport 16 N959 of N65 fell into German hands shortly after it had been used to burn a balloon on 22 May 1916. Réservat escaped from captivity in March 1917 and made his way back to France. Four of the Nieuport's Le Prieur rockets are still in their interplane strut-mounted tubes, and the aeroplane's elaborate gunsight is also of interest. (Greg VanWyngarden)

the rocket's heat and flame to ignite, ending in a fiery *Götterdämmerung* for the offending 'sausage'.

Although the Nieuport 11 and 16 *Bébés* had a relatively short period of prominence over the Western Front, they influenced a number of more successful derivatives to come – on both sides of the lines – and they continued to give good service over other fronts, including Russia, the Balkans and Italy, as late as 1917. A total of 1,000 Nieuport 11s and 16s were produced in France, another 646 Nieuport 11s were built under licence in Italy (including 450 by Macchi-Nieuport, which designated them 1100s, and 93 by the *Officine Elettro-Ferroviarie* in Milan)

NIEUPORT 11/16 LEWIS MOUNTING

The Nieuport 11 and 16 usually carried a 7.7mm (0.303in) Lewis Mk 1 machine gun above the upper wing, employing a variety of mountings that allowed it to be pulled back and down for reloading. The Moreau mount shown here was seen in many Nieuport units, including *'l'Escadrille Américaine'* N124 – a similar arrangement was produced by Vasily V. Yordan for Russian *Bébés* in the Eighth Field Army. A number of enterprising French, British and Belgian pilots created twin mountings. The rail-based Foster mount, devised in No. 11 Sqn, became standard for the RFC. Finally, at least one Nieuport 11 and several 16s had Lewis guns synchronized by Alkan-Hamy interrupter gear.

and about 200 were licence produced by the Russian Duks, Mosca, Anatra and Shchetinin factories. A number of the Duks-produced Nieuport 11s were built with pine rather than spruce frameworks, adding some 66lb (30kg) in weight, to the detriment of performance.

FOKKER E I

The Fokker monoplanes embodied a curious mix of the visionary and reactionary that characterized Anthony Fokker himself, and the German air service, throughout the war. In Fokker's case, at least, one can find an explanation for the paradox – inventive though he could be, he was first and foremost a businessman. Even while he experimented with new structures and devices, his practical application of them was ultimately aimed at selling aeroplanes to *Idflieg*.

Based on the Morane-Saulnier shoulder-winged Type H and L monoplanes in fundamental concept, the Fokker E I was aerodynamically superior and structurally more advanced, with its welded steel tube fuselage structure. That difference was most marked in comparisons with the Pfalz *Eindeckers* that were produced to supplement the Fokkers' never-adequate numbers. Essentially licence-built copies of the Morane-Saulnier H – they were even called 'Moranes' by the pilots who flew them – the Pfalz E I and its progeny used the same wood and fabric construction as the French originals. And although comparable to the Fokkers in weight and speed, they were criticized by their pilots for being less manoeuvrable in the air and by the mechanics for being equally sluggish to manhandle on the ground.

FOKKER *EINDECKER* FUSELAGE GUN

The most-used armament on Fokker *Eindeckers* was the Spandau-produced 7.92mm LMG 08, using the mechanical push rod interrupter gear devised by Anthony Fokker and his design team. By late 1916 this system had been rendered obsolete by the introduction of an improved electrical system, adapted to fit the 7.92mm LMG 08/15.

Pfalz E I 479/15 prepares for take-off from Vilna on the Eastern Front. Closer copies of Morane-Saulnier designs than Fokker's monoplane, the Pfalz *Eindeckers* did not perform or handle as well as the Fokkers and most were relegated to sectors other than the Western Front. (Jon Guttman)

Notwithstanding the Fokker *Eindecker*'s advanced fuselage and tail surfaces, its wing followed the pre-war formula of having two I-section main spars supporting poplar wood ribs to produce a fabric-covered flying surface that was parallel in chord, featured raked tips and was thin in cross section for flexibility. Lateral control was by wing warping, with the rear set of cables played via pulleys fitted to the rear of the upper fuselage and aft undercarriage pylons to the cockpit, where they were connected to the control column.

The cowling cheeks aft of the engine on the first six E Is, armed with Parabellum machine guns, took on a more squared-off look than the smoothly curved cowl 'cheeks' on the Fokker A I (M8), A II (M 5L) and A III (M 5K) in order to accommodate the starboard ammunition bin and the port bin for collecting empty belts. After Fokker decided to adopt the LMG 08 as standard armament and relocate the empty belt bin from under the cowl cheek to inside the fuselage, the port cowl cheek reverted to its original curved shape.

Oblt Kurt Student and his groundcrew ready their Fokker E I for take-off from Leffincourt. Mudguards have been added to the undercarriage in an attempt to keep debris from being kicked up into the engine. (Lance Bronnenkant)

Among the accessories that might or might not appear on the *Eindeckers* was a windscreen and an adjustable headrest. The latter, consisting of a pad on a tripod steel tube pedestal, was intended not for comfort, but for the pilot to brace his head against to steady himself while aiming his vibrating aeroplane, and the machine gun fixed to it. Some German airmen modified the windscreen and most dispensed with the headrest.

E II

During the course of early *Eindecker* production Fokker did some minor refining of his basic formula, leading at first to the E II (M14). This replaced the 80hp Oberursel U 0 rotary engine with a nine-cylinder 100hp U 1. Although some 30 per cent more powerful and more reliable than its precursor, the engine was also larger and heavier, necessitating a lengthened fuselage – the French noted a 30cm increase on captured examples – and relocation of the cockpit and wings 16cm closer to the engine to compensate for the changed aerodynamic centre of gravity, along with an 8–10cm enlargement in cowling diameter.

Fokker made little distinction between the E I and E II on the production line, recording a collective total of 85 before the E III replaced them both. Historian Peter M. Grosz estimated the E II as representing anywhere from 24 to 36 of that number. Both scouts had their 98-litre main fuel tank and oil tank located in front of the pilot, where the installation of the machine gun led to their having to compete for space with ammunition and the interrupter gear. The E II had a 22-litre auxiliary fuel tank aft of the pilot as well.

E III

The only major difference between the Fokker E II and the E III was that the latter featured a new petrol tank aft of the cockpit and a modified front reserve tank that freed up more space under the cowling for the ammunition arrangement. Otherwise, E IIIs and the five last E IIs in the second production batch were indistinguishable. A wing-mounted compass was added to E IIIs of the third production batch.

Fokker E II 71/15, assigned to KEK Cunel, was written off in this landing mishap. It is thought that the aeroplane was flown by Ltn Hans Berr prior to its demise. (Lance Bronnenkant)

FOKKER E II *EINDECKER* COCKPIT

1. 7.92mm LMG 08/15 machine gun
2. Fuel gauge
3. Ring and bead gunsight
4. Fuel tank cap
5. Empty ammunition belt guide
6. Ammunition feed
7. Fuel control lever
8. Tachometer
9. Magneto switch
10. Spent cartridge bin
11. Ammunition box

12. Air pressure gauge
13. Oil pulsator
14. Fuel system cocks
15. Altimeter
16. Air pressure hand pump for fuel system
17. Sliding hatches (port and starboard) – opened for better view
18. Hinged floor panels – opened for better view
19. Rudder bar control
20. Foot rests

21. Machine gun fire button
22. Control column grip
23. Control column
24. Seat
25. Cocking lever for LMG 08 machine gun
26. Fuel on/off switch
27. Carburettor adjustment handle
28. Knee grip
29. Control column lock

So swift was the refining process of the armed *Eindeckers* that the E III was replacing the E II on the Fokker production line in September 1915 – little more than a month after Immelmann's and Boelcke's first successes in the E I. With 268 built for the German army, 14 additional units produced for the navy and 18 for export to Austria-Hungary and Turkey, the E III was the principal variant to see action and the real source of the term 'Fokker Scourge' as its numbers proliferated along the front.

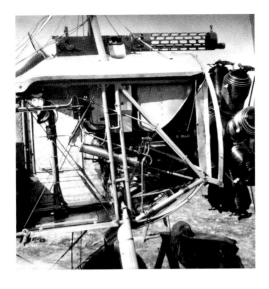

A Fokker E III of KEK Cunel provides an interior close-up of the cockpit, including the interrupter gear that was the key to the fighter's success for almost a year. (David Méchin)

On 8 April 1916 Fokker E III 210/16 landed on the wrong side of the lines and fell into British hands intact. In their evaluaton of the 'scourge' at Upavon, the British reported, among other things, that the fuselage framework was steel with 'brazed joints – no sprockets', and that the aeroplane had 'double flap doors in the floor between the pilot's knees and shutters on either side under the wings, all of which can be worked by the pilot for getting a better view'. All wing connections, they noted, were 'fitted with quick, detachable joints for rapid dismantling'. Fuel consumption was gauged at 9.5 gallons an hour and its three gallons of oil consumed at 2.3 gallons per hour. During a speed test on 31 May the aeroplane attained 86.4mph at 1,210rpm, with a minimum speed of 50mph. During a steep dive the E III reached 115mph and recovered with 'complete ease'.

Fokker E III 422/15, representing the principal *Eindecker* production variant, was also attached to KEK Cunel. German pilots usually restricted the application of personal markings to the wheel hubs of their aeroplanes in 1916. (Archives Départmentales de la Moselle)

In general the British reported the E III to be unstable 'laterally, longitudinally and directionally' and 'tiring to fly in all but still air'. They also claimed that the 'machine persistently flies right wing-down, which is impossible to cure without setting springs to control the stick'. With an undercarriage track of 6ft 8in, however, landing was easy.

	E I	E II	E III
Dimensions			
Wingspan	29ft 4.5in	32ft 11.6in	32ft 11.6in
Wing area	150.69sq ft	150.69sq ft	150.69sq ft
Length	22ft 9.5in	23ft 9.5in	23ft 9.5in
Height	8ft 3in	8ft 0.5in	8ft 0.5in
Armament	1 x 7.92mm LMG 08 machine gun (all three variants)		
Weight (lb)			
Empty	788	878	880
Loaded	1,239	1,232	1,342
Performance			
Engine	Oberursel U 0 7-cyl 80hp	Oberursel U I 9-cyl 100hp	Oberursel U I 9-cyl 100hp
Maximum speed	82mph	87mph	87.5mph
Climb to 3,280ft	5 min	-	-
Climb to 2,000ft	20 min	-	-
Climb to 9,840ft	30 min	-	-
Service ceiling (ft)	10,000	11,500	11,500
Endurance	1.5 hrs	1.5 hrs	2.5 hrs

THE CELLON E III

In May–June 1912, Austro-Hungarian Hptm István Petróczy von Petrócz replaced the fabric on an Etrich Taube with a transparent celluloid derivative called emallit. He subsequently reported that only the engine and framework were dimly visible at an altitude of 700ft, and that the entire aeroplane became invisible at 900ft to 1,200ft. In 1913–14 a German, Anton Knubel, similarly covered a Taube in transparent material for comparison with another one covered with blue-grey camouflage fabric.

In 1916 the Germans pursued further experiments in this early form of aerial 'stealth technology' using a celluloid-like material called *'durchsichtige Bespannung'* (see-through covering) Cellon, which had seen some use in automobiles as a glass substitute. The aeroplanes that were covered in it ranged from the giant VGO and Linke-Hoffmann R I bombers to Aviatik, Albatros C I and Rumpler C I two-seaters, down to three Fokker E IIIs. An intriguing suggestion of frontline use emerges from a report by

No. 16 Sqn RFC on 9 July 1916, which notes that 'a transparent German aeroplane marked with red crosses was pursued by French machines in the Somme area'.

Cellon was wetted before application, contracting and tautening as it dried. In practice, however, the Germans noted that 'during longer periods of rain or damp weather the covering becomes so loose that it would be better not to fly such aircraft'. Unlike celluloid, Cellon did not burn or shatter, but its evaluators stated that while 'the covering itself is strong, should shrapnel go through the wing the whole sheet would tear to pieces'.

Photographs of Fokker E III 369/15, both on the ground and in the air, revealed the ultimate problem with Cellon *D-Bespannung*, as expressed in the test results of July 1916:

> In clear weather, the aircraft is more difficult to spot, but in cloudy weather it appears just as dark as other aircraft. In the sunshine, the pilot and observer are unpleasantly blinded by the reflections.

Transparency was clearly not the best way to conceal an aeroplane, and by the end of the year the Germans had standardized fabric preprinted with multiple irregular hexagons as their principal means of camouflage.

This photograph of Fokker E III 369/15 on the ground in July 1916 shows just how effective its experimental skin of Cellon *D-Bespannung* was at reducing its visibility in the air. From some angles it is clear, but from others the sun reflects off it, thus making its presence all the more obvious. (Greg VanWyngarden)

E IV

While the Fokker factory was well engaged in filling *Idflieg* orders for the E III, in November 1915 Kreuzer and his staff built what they hoped would maintain the *Eindecker's* edge against any new opposition the Allies might devise. The powerplant of the Fokker M 15, or E IV, was essentially two Oberursel U 0 rotary engines bolted together to produce a 14-cylinder double row version with an output of 160hp. In anticipation of the vibration the motor might also produce, support bearings were added to the engine mounts, extending to the front. Slotted holes were added to the cowling face to enhance cooling. To compensate for the engine's weight, the

Probably photographed being prepared for take-off from Sivry by its regular pilot, Oblt Ernst *Freiherr* von Althaus, Fokker E IV 183/15 shows the twin-row Oberursel U III engine with fretted cowling and front 'spider' support and the faired-over twin machine guns that distinguished this disappointing attempt to extend the supremacy of the *Eindecker*. (Greg VanWyngarden)

fuselage was enlarged to 7.5m (24ft 8in) and the height increased to 2.75m (9ft 2in) to accommodate reinforced landing gear struts and the upper wing support pylon. Wingspan and chord were unchanged from the E III.

Armament on the E IV was increased to two 7.92mm LMG 08 machine guns in the upper cowl, with an improved ammunition feed system. As with Britain's first twin-gun fighter, the Sopwith Camel (introduced more than a year later), the E IV partially enclosed its guns in a humped upper decking that extended aft of the cockpit, tapering down into the fuselage.

Although faster in level flight and stronger and more heavily armed than its predecessors, the Fokker E IV also proved to be less manoeuvrable and its engine less reliable. For one thing, the aft row of cylinders could not get as much cooling air as the front row, making it prone to overheating. Over time performance deteriorated, especially rate-of-climb and control responsiveness.

Oswald Boelcke made an official report of these shortcomings, noting a loss of 100rpm in the course of regular service use and an inability to make quick turns without stopping the engine, at the cost of height. He also stated that he had lost several opportunities to bring down Nieuports because of the E IV's inferior rate-of-climb. Boelcke concluded with the suggestion that biplanes would be better suited to maintaining Germany's edge in the face of improving Allied fighters.

One E IV, 122/16, was experimentally armed with three machine guns. After its first evaluation flights, the fighter was briefly used at the front by Ltn Parschau in November 1915. There is no evidence that it was flown operationally before it reverted to twin weapons, with the extra gun position faired over.

A total of 49 Fokker E IVs had been produced by March 1916, one of which went to the navy. Largely as a consequence of Boelcke's harshly critical report, an order for 20 more was cancelled in April. Fokker would not mass-produce another monoplane until the E V, featuring a cantilever structure parasol wing, in 1918.

THE STRATEGIC SITUATION

WESTERN FRONT IN 1915–16

Since the dramatic events of the war's first several months, culminating in September 1914 with the Allied halting of the German offensive in France in the First Battle of the Marne, and the German containment of the Russian onslaught in the East at Tannenberg, efforts by both sides on the Western Front had effectively come to naught. The ultimate outcome by the beginning of 1915 was an almost solid pair of lines with a desolate no man's land in between, snaking and zig-zagging their way across France from the North Sea to Switzerland, along which soldiers of both sides dug in to seek shelter from one another's artillery. Soon both sides established in-depth defences dominated by a series of trench lines, through which neither side seemed able to make significant headway.

The Austro-Hungarian conquest of Serbia (on the second attempt), Russian success against the Austro-Hungarians in Galicia, the Ottoman Empire's entry into the war with the Central Powers in November 1914 and Italy's joining the Allies in May 1915, only to see its first offensive swiftly halted by the Austro-Hungarian army, had virtually no effect on the overall stalemate that prevailed in the West.

While both sides sought a means of breaking the deadlock, aeroplanes played their part, gathering intelligence and harassing the enemy with bombs or flechettes. Aerial combat slowly proliferated, but it was not until Roland Garros' brief run of success in

After arriving at Jametz Oblt Oswald Boelcke swiftly recognized the flaws in the *Sperre* strategy for defending airspace over Verdun. He demanded – and got – a freer hand to use his fighters, and established a more forward base at Sivry, from which he could respond quickly to telephoned reports of enemy activity over the front. (Lance Bronnenkant)

April 1915, followed by the unleashing of the Fokker E I in July, that the first halting steps were made in the quest for air superiority. The next year would see efforts to break the stalemate on the Western Front resume with a vengeance – and with them, the first serious attempts to achieve control of the sky above the battlefield.

That grand effort began on the morning of 21 February 1916 when the old fortresses around Verdun-sur-Meuse came under a ten-hour artillery bombardment, followed by an offensive involving some 150,000 German troops. The architect of the offensive, Chief of Staff Erich von Falkenhayn, hoped to overrun the weakened defences in that sector from three sides. After some initial successes in the first few days, however, the French XX Corps arrived to bolster the 30,000 shaken defenders of the XXX Corps, joined on the 25th by Gen Henri Philippe Pétain's *IIe Armée*. By the 29th German momentum was faltering and 90,000 French reinforcements, as well as 23,000 tons of ammunition, were arriving via their sole rail line connection through Bar-le-Duc.

At that point Falkenhayn altered his strategy from one of breakthrough to one of attrition, counting on his forces' superior positioning and firepower to bleed the French army white. What ensued was the longest and most agonizing battle of the war. Concurrently, Verdun also became the crucible of the war's first deliberate effort to achieve control above the battlefield through the massed concentration of air assets.

On the eve of the commencement of the Verdun campaign *Inspektor Major* Friedrich Stempel, the staff officer in charge of aviation to Prince Rupprecht of Bavaria's 6. *Armee*, had formed specialized units called *Kampfeinsitzer Kommandos*, or KEKs, consisting of two to four Fokker or Pfalz *Eindeckers*. Detached from their escort duties in reconnaissance or artillery spotting *Feldflieger Abteilungen*, or from bombing *Kampfgeschwader der Obersten der Heeresleitung*, or *Kagohls*, the KEK pilots were tasked with *Luftwachtdienst* (aerial guard duty) – essentially a roving commission to roam the front and eliminate whatever Allied aeroplanes they encountered.

At the start of the Verdun offensive the staff officer in charge of the German 5. *Armee*'s air arm, Hptm Wilhelm Haehnelt, had 168 operational aircraft. Of those, only 21 were Fokker and Pfalz monoplanes, which operated either in *Flieger Abteilungen*, *Kagohls* or in two- to four-aeroplane KEKs based at Avillers, Jametz and Cunel. Haehnelt's original strategy was for the fighters to constantly patrol the front, forming a *Sperre*, or 'blockade', against any French aircraft trying to penetrate airspace over the 5. *Armee*. This task was impossible for the limited number of armed scouts available to him, making it necessary to supplement their ranks with two-seaters drawn from the *Kagohls*. Even then, constant patrolling took its toll on the *Eindeckers'* rotary engines, which could not stand up to the same sustained activity that their more conventional water-cooled contemporaries could.

While the French army reeled under the shock of the German onslaught on 21 February, its air arm had the best of that first day, suffering two men wounded and four injured, but claiming eight German aircraft destroyed, of which half were confirmed. The French continued to more than hold their own until 11 March, when Oblt Oswald Boelcke, detached from FFA 62 for duty at Verdun but sidelined for a while by what he called 'some stupid intestinal trouble', reported to KEK Jametz. Upon arrival, he promptly obtained Hptm Haehnelt's permission to establish a new *Kommando* of his own, equipped with two and later three Fokkers, at Sivry, north of Verdun.

It did not take long for Boelcke, whose score then stood at nine, to recognize the inherent flaws in the *Sperre* concept – and, as would recur several times in future, he devised his own solution. With Sivry lying just 11km behind the front, he established direct contact with a forward observation post that would telephone him to report the approach of any French aeroplane. Upon being alerted, Boelcke or one of his men could be scrambled to intercept the intruder, thus conserving the aeroplane's fuel and lubricant and the pilot's energy. The greater efficiency of Boelcke's tactics produced dramatic results over the next few days, hampering French efforts to reconnoitre the sector with an effectiveness that established the fundamental model for German fighter defences for the rest of the war.

Boelcke gets a visit from *Kronprinz* Wilhelm of Prussia, commander of the 5. *Armee*. Sivry was not far from the crown prince's headquarters at Stenay, and the two men became good friends. (David Méchin)

The success of the German combination of *Sperre* flights and Boelcke's alert system for interfering with French reconnaissance missions caught the attention of Gen Pétain. Summoning his chief of air operations, Cmdt Jean Baptiste Marie Charles, Baron de Tricornot, Marquis de Rose, to his headquarters on 28 February, he issued an order that virtually defined the air war for the next two and a half years – 'De Rose, I am blind! Sweep the skies for me!'

Pétain certainly did not have to tell de Rose twice. One of the first French officers to embrace the aeroplane as a weapon, he had trained on Caudrons at Pau to qualify for his civilian licence on 12 December 1910. The pioneer aviator was subsequently awarded Military Brevet No. 1 on 7 February 1911. A major in charge of the *Ve Armée*'s air assets when the Nieuport 10 began reaching the

front, de Rose ordered MS12 to replace its Morane-Saulnier L two-seater parasol monoplanes with single-seat variants of the sesquiplanes. On 23 September 1915 the unit was fully re-equipped and redesignated *escadrille de chasse* (hunting or pursuit squadron) N12, thus becoming the first single-seat fighter squadron in history.

Until sufficient numbers of Nieuport 11 *Bébés* became available to replace the 10s, they were supplemented by a handful of deflector-equipped Morane-Saulnier Nm monoplanes. It was in one of the latter that N12's unruly but aggressive star turn,

Adj Jean Navarre, brought down LVG C I 523/15 of FFA 33 on 26 October, resulting in Uffz Otto Gerold and Ltn Paul Bucholtz being made PoWs. Gerold died of his wounds shortly thereafter, however. This was Navarre's third victory, as he had scored twice before while flying the Morane-Saulnier L.

N12 had received its complement of *Bébés*, as had several other designated fighter units along the front, by the time the Battle of Verdun began.

In direct response to Pétain's order, de Rose concentrated his fighter *escadrilles* around the Verdun-Bar-le-Duc sector in provisional hunting groups, or *groupements de chasse provisoires*. One consisted of N65 and N67 supporting the *IIe Armée* from Bar-le-Duc, with N23 serving as a reserve at Vadelaincourt. N15 and N69, also at Bar-le-Duc, were tasked with driving off German aircraft in the *Xe Armée* sector. N57 soon joined the effort from Lemmes.

Instead of conducting barrage patrols in certain assigned sectors, de Rose ordered all of these units to aggressively seek out and destroy any enemy aeroplane they saw. Ever the officer to lead by example, the 39-year-old de Rose flew his share of line patrols in his own Nieuport 11 N536, with a rose emblazoned on the fuselage side.

By the spring of 1916 battle lines had more or less been drawn in the air as well as on the ground. While both sides focused primarily on protecting their own reconnaissance aeroplanes, as well as denying the sky to the other's, the French experimented with various tactics for using the massed scout units they had assembled at Verdun. The Germans, however, tried to make the most efficient use of the smaller fighter formations they had stationed in the area to oppose their French counterparts. Success was usually determined by the aggressiveness and skill of the individual but, as the battle progressed, tactical acumen, acquired by hard experience, began to dictate the conduct of the struggle in the air as the combatants evolved and refined the embryonic elements of fighter doctrine.

THE COMBATANTS

AÉRONAUTIQUE MILITAIRE

In spite of the innovative pioneering done by various individuals and manufacturers, the French air service (*Aéronautique Militaire*) began 1916 with a woeful preponderance of obsolescent aircraft, and a paucity of fighters to protect them. Of the 675 aeroplanes operational in February 1916, 101 were Maurice Farman 11 pushers, 167 were Caudron G 4s, 120 were Nieuport 10s and only 90 were Nieuport 11s.

Apart from the daredevils, usually with pre-war experience, who enthusiastically set out to develop the fighter, France's first generation of *chasse* pilots had to be winnowed out from those undergoing standard training on reconnaissance and bomber aircraft. There were literally two schools of thought toward getting these noephytes into the sky. At Pau one could start out on the ground in *'rouleurs'* – Blériot XIs with their wings clipped short, powered by 25hp to 45hp engines. After getting his first phase of instruction, the trainee was sent on his way to putter around the airfield while his instructor, or *moniteur*, judged how much control he was exercising over his *'Pingouin'*. Once the student had built up some confidence on these flight simulators, he was given further instructions for actual flight in Blériots with 100hp engines. After circling over the field, the pilot was given a final test involving a 150km circuit that, if successful, would earn him his brevet, or flying certificate.

An alternative to Blériot *rouleur* training was dual instruction in Caudron G 3s at Avord. Either way, once the pilot had soloed and qualified for his brevet he underwent more advanced training, often determined by the *moniteur's* appraisal of how steady or dexterous his flying had been in that last test. Pilots judged best suited for reconnaissance

work trained in Caudron G 4s or Maurice Farmans, while bomber pilots trained in Voisins. Nieuport 10s and a succession of obsolescent single-seaters would later serve to train a growing cadre of *chasse* pilots once that speciality was established.

After advanced instruction, including gunnery at Cazeaux, the pilot was sent to the *Groupe Division d'Entrainement* (GDE) at Plessis-Belleville, where he would continue training until he received his assignment to an operational squadron. Once at the front, a bomber or reconnaissance pilot might come to display aggressive traits that could lead his *chef de l'escadrille* to recommend a transfer to a *chasse* outfit. Just such behaviour – including the destruction of an enemy aeroplane during an unauthorized sortie on 31 July 1915 – inspired the commander of Voisin-equipped bombing *escadrille* VB106 to order Adj Charles Nungesser confined to quarters for eight days, after which he awarded him the *Croix de Guerre* and sent him off for *chasse* training. When Nungesser returned to the front, it would be with N65, with whom he could – and would – raise hell in a Nieuport 16.

Another demonstrated candidate for scouts was Sgt Jean Chaput of C28. On 12 June 1915, while flying an obsolete Caudron G 3, he and his observer were credited with forcing a Fokker monoplane – probably an A III – to land near Esnes for his first credited victory. On 10 July, still in a G 3, he was reportedly attacked by a Fokker monoplane that, at the time, would have been flown by Ltn Kurt Wintgens of FFA 6b. Chaput's carbine was hit and disabled, his left hand shot through, an interplane strut smashed and a contusion to his chest caused by a bullet richocheting off his just-awarded *Médaille Militaire*, and another stopped by his pocket notebook and cigarette case. Somehow Chaput managed to escape his assailant and bring his observer back unharmed.

After his return from hospital Chaput's pleas for his own scout were rewarded on 7 January 1916, when he was sent to train on Nieuport 11s at Le Bourget and then assigned to N31 at Bar-le-Duc on 1 March. On the 13th he was assigned Nieuport 11 N860, and after two familiarization flights he commenced flying combat sorties, attacking an LVG without result on the 17th.

Nieuport 10 N265 at the aviation school at Pau. As Nieuport 11s and 16s replaced them in the scout role, single-seat Nieuport 10s became advanced trainers to introduce budding fighter pilots to the sesquiplane's flight characteristics. (SHDA B88.3394)

This typical *escadrille* line-up shows aircraft of the American volunteer unit N124 at Behonne on 14 May 1916, including, from right, Nieuport 11 N1116 flown by Sgt Norman Prince, Nieuport 16 N1131 of Sgt Elliott C. Cowdin, Nieuport 11 1164 of Capt Georges Thenault, Nieuport 11 N1247 of Sgt H. Clyde Balseley, Nieuport 11 N1148 of Sgt Victor Chapman, Nieuport 11 1286 of Sgt Lawrence Rumsey and Nieuport 11 N1292 of Cpl James McConnell. (George H. Williams via Greg VanWyngarden)

When the Battle of Verdun began, the *Aéronautique Militaire* distributed its fighter units along the front, with N23 and N67 near the fortress, N12 attached to the *Armée de l'Aisne*, N37 with the *Armée de l'Argonne*, N3 with the *Armée de Picardie*, N15, N57 and N69 with the *Xe Armée*, and N26 and N65 in support of the Belgian army. Upon being assigned to the sector, however, Cmdt de Rose redistributed them to concentrate in the Verdun-Bar-le-Duc area as a *groupements de combat provisoire*, the nucleus of which consisted of N65 and N67 at Bar-le-Duc. As of 15 March those two were joined by N15 and N69, while N23 stood in reserve at Vadelaincourt, N37 swept the Argonne from its aerodrome at Brocourt and N57 arrived at Lemmes.

Revising their orders from flying barrage patrols over specifically assigned sectors to concentrating on actively seizing local superiority over specific points on the front had a favourable effect on the morale of the budding *pilotes de chasse*.

Besides French airmen, adventurous volunteers from other nations such as Russia, Switzerland, China and Japan began turning up in the squadrons, including *escadrilles de chasse*. On 16 April a new scout unit, N124, was formed around a spirited contingent of volunteers from the neutral United States. Dubbed *l'Escadrille des Américains* – a sobriquet that would later lead to some diplomatic embarrassment, eventually resulting in its being rechristened *l'Escadrille Lafayette* – N124 had three Nieuport 16s and three 11s on strength when it flew its first combat sorties from Luxeuil-les-Bains on 13 May. Just five days later one of its members, Cpl Kiffin Rockwell, was credited with a two-seater for its first victory. The next day, 19 May, N124 was transferred from its relatively quiet sector to Behonne, near Bar-le-Duc, to participate in the 'main event' over Verdun.

ROYAL NAVAL AIR SERVICE

Originally a branch of the RFC, the RNAS became a separate entity in the summer of 1914, just before war broke out. Although both services had experimented with mounting machine guns on pusher aircraft, RNAS pilots such as Cdr Charles Rumney Samson were

ALBERT DEULLIN

Although Jean Navarre dominated the headlines as the 'Sentinel of Verdun', Albert Deullin contributed his own small share to the aerial struggle. More importantly, like his German counterpart Oswald Boelcke, he wrote down the lessons derived from his experience and this formed the basis of future French fighter doctrine.

Albert Louis Deullin was born in Epernay (Marne) on 24 August 1890 and entered military service with the 8e Régiment de Dragons on 1 October 1910. He was placed on inactive duty as a non-commissioned officer two years later, but was mobilized with the 31e Régiment de Dragons on 2 August 1914. Promoted to sous-lieutenant in December, Deullin decided to forsake horses for flying machines in April 1915, earning military pilot's brevet No. 988 on 26 May and being assigned to escadrille MF62 on 2 July.

During a photo-reconnaissance mission 30km into enemy territory on 10 February 1916 Deullin and his observer, Capitaine René Colcomb, were attacked by an enemy aeroplane, which they drove down to a forced landing, then returned through a 30-minute barrage of anti-aircraft fire. Besides credit for his first victory, Deullin was cited the next day for the Médaille de Saint Georges. Soon afterward he was promoted to lieutenant and transferred to N3, where he quickly mastered the Nieuport 11 and joined that escadrille's elite circle. On 19 March he was credited with an enemy aeroplane destroyed, and his subsequent scoring included Fokker Eindeckers on 31 March and 30 April. On 4 June he was made a Chevalier de la Légion d'Honneur, with the following citation:

'Pilot with exceptional initiative and sang-froid, endlessly seeking battle against enemy aeroplanes. Wounded on 2 April during the course of aerial combat, he returned to his Escadrille before being completely rehabilitated, and since his return has had 12 auspicious combats. On 30 April 1916 he attacked point blank an enemy aeroplane and downed it in front of our trenches. Already cited twice in army orders.'

On 26 June Deullin became an ace when he destroyed a kite balloon in flames over Péronne. Flying Nieuport 17s and SPAD VIIs, he brought his total to 11 on 10 February 1917, by which time N3 was one of four escadrilles in Groupe de Combat (GC) 12 'Les Cigognes' – each unit marked its aeroplanes with a stork emblem depicted in a different attitude of flight. On 22 February Lt Deullin was given command of another 'stork' unit, N73, with which he added a further eight victories to his tally during the course of the year.

On 7 February 1918 the redesignated SPA73 was transferred from GC12 to the new GC19, operating from the 14th onward with SPA85, SPA95 and SPA96. GC19's newly assigned and promoted commander was Capt Deullin, who continued to fly combat missions and downed an Albatros east of Montdidier on 19 May for his 20th, and final, confirmed victory. On 23 June he was made an Officier de la Légion d'Honneur, in addition to which he held the Croix de Guerre with 14 palmes. Although Deullin survived the war, he was killed on 29 May 1923 while test flying an aeroplane prototype at Villacoublay airfield.

Albert Deullin (Christophe Cony)

more decisive in coming to favour single-seat tractor aircraft as the ideal weapon. By July 1915 Nieuport 10 two-seaters and single-seat Bristol Scouts armed with overwing Lewis guns were operating over the Dardanelles, and when the Nieuport 11 *Bébé* entered production the RNAS made substantial orders for it from November onwards.

By late summer 1915 the RNAS had six squadrons, two of which were fighter units, in the Dunkirk area, as well as two in Dover, all under the command of Wg Capt Charles L. Lambe. At that time what the RFC called a squadron the RNAS called a wing, whose six-aeroplane squadrons corresponded to an RFC flight. By December Lambe had obtained the Admiralty's approval to form two more wings, each comprising four squadrons.

One of Lambe's Dunkirk-based units, No. 1 Wing at St Pol-sur-Mer, included a specialized fighter element, 'A' Sqn, equipped with Nieuport 10s and 11s. This squadron produced what has retrospectively been acknowledged as the RNAS' first ace in the person of Flt Sub-Lt Redford Henry Mulock from Manitoba, Canada. Having already demonstrated his aggressive approach to patrolling, reconnoitring and bombing, 'Red' Mulock joined the wing in July 1915 and was credited with his first victory – a two-seater 'out of control' (OOC) near the Houthulst Forest – on 30 December. Flying Nieuport 11 3977, he forced a two-seater to land near Westende on 24 January 1916, and was credited with another OOC near Nieuport two days later.

Matching Mulock's zeal once Nieuport 11s became available was Australian Flt Lt Roderic Stanley Dallas, who opened his account with a two-seater 'OOC' near Middelkerke on 22 April 1916, and a floatplane destroyed off Blankenberghe on 20 May. On 21 May Mulock, in Nieuport 3992, drove two enemy two-seaters down OOC off Nieuwport, bringing his total to five, while Dallas downed another north of Dunkirk. The RNAS standard for counting enemy aeroplanes 'forced to land' or seen 'out of control' made a dubious criterion for aerial victories. In Mulock's case they

Although this aeroplane looks like a Nieuport 11, 3956 was in fact one of ten Nieuport 17Bs ordered by the RNAS in August 1916 that were equipped with lighter-weight 80hp Le Rhône 9C engines for greater range, as well as overwing Lewis mountings and no headrests. The French produced their own 80hp Nieuport 17s under the designation of Nieuport 21. Nieuport 3956 was marked *Binky* while with 3 Naval Squadron at St Pol in January 1917, and it subsequently served in other units before being retired in May. (Colin Owers)

reflected an overall élan that, combined with his equally relentless bombing sorties, earned him the Distinguished Service Order in June.

That same month 'A' Sqn moved closer to the front, at Furnes, and was furnished solely with Nieuport 11s. Known as the 'Detached Squadron', it was the first uniformly equipped unit in the RNAS, and the forebear of a distinguished pantheon of naval fighter squadrons that would gain renown flying various Sopwith scouts in the year to come.

ROYAL FLYING CORPS

The RFC had had scout pilots – in the sense that they flew single-seaters over the lines to scout out the enemy – since its first operations in France. Its early air fighters, however, were those who took matters into their own hands, as Lts Hubert D, Harvey-Kelly and W. H. C. Mansfield did when they attacked a Rumpler Taube with pistols on 25 August 1914.

The first aeroplane to bear the designation of 'fighting aircraft' in regular RFC service was a two-seat pusher, the Vickers FB 5, followed by the Royal Aircraft Factory's larger 'Farman Experimental' FE 2b. Each was armed with a Lewis gun manned by the observer up front, to which the FE later added a second Lewis on a pole mounting that gave the observer a precarious means of firing over the upper wing and propeller in the event of an enemy attack from behind.

Some enterprising individuals, however, experimented with arming single-seat tractor scouts. No. 6 Sqn, which supplemented its BE 2c two-seaters with a scout or two, boasted two such characters. On 10 May 1915 Capt Louis A. Strange went up in the squadron's newly delivered Martinsyde S 1 scout with a Lewis gun installed above the upper wing to attack an Aviatik, only to suffer a jam. Since the gun could not be pulled down, he stood up and spent some ten minutes trying to free the magazine – until the Martinsyde suddenly stalled and yawed, throwing him out of the cockpit. At that point Strange's curses at the ammunition drum's refusal to come loose turned to prayers that it would not, as he clung to it for dear life and swung his body about in a desperate effort to regain the cockpit. On the third try he succeeded, and having spun down 7,000ft he managed to right the Martinsyde within the remaining 1,500ft.

Upon Strange's return to base his commanding officer admonished him for the 'unnecessary damage' he had done to to the instruments and seat in the course of his kicking about! Strange spent the next 12 hours sleeping off that harrowing ordeal, about which he lived to write in his *Recollections of an Airman* in 1933.

Besides the Martinsyde, No. 6 Sqn also received some FE 2bs in May to act as escorts for its two-seaters. Then, on 3 June, another of the unit's pilots, Capt Lanoe G. Hawker, wrote in a letter home that 'I have a beautiful new toy – a new Bristol Scout that goes at 80mph and climbs at 500ft or 600ft a minute! I'm having a machine gun fitted to see how they like it'. The gun, firing slightly downward and to the left on a framework devised by Hawker and Air Mechanic Ernest J. Elton, was hardly a 'point and shoot' arrangement, yet Hawker managed to drive an LVG down OOC with it on 21 June and destroyed two Albatros two-seaters four days later – the latter action resulted in Hawker being awarded the first Victoria Cross for aerial combat. He scored his next three

A134 was one of several Nieuport 16s flown by Lt Albert Ball while assigned to No. 11 Sqn RFC. On 2 July he used it to bring down a Roland C II and an Aviatik, and the next day he installed Le Prieur rockets to its wings for an unsuccessful attempt at a *Drachen*. (Bruce/Leslie collection)

victories – including a Fokker *Eindecker* on 11 August 1915 – in FE 2b 4227, but claimed a two-seater for his seventh in Bristol Scout 1611 on 7 September.

These extraordinary cases notwithstanding, until suitable British single-seat designs were developed the RFC purchased armed scouts from France, starting with the Morane-Saulnier Nm, which its airmen dubbed the 'Bullet', complete with the fleetingly innovative but now obsolescent airscrew deflectors. Although it did not use the Nieuport 11, the RFC did deploy modest numbers of its more powerful descendant, the Nieuport 16. Initially, these scouts were assigned, like the Fokkers, to reconnaissance units in small escorting flights similar to the Germans' first use of Fokker *Eindeckers* in their *Feldflieger Abteilungen*.

Among such units was No. 11 Sqn, an FE 2b-equipped unit that had a flight of three Nieuport 16s whose pilots included a young hotspur named Albert Ball. It was also a mechanic in that detachment, Sgt R. G. Foster, who devised a curved rail mounting that would allow the gun to be pulled down into a vertical position in front of the pilot, easing the chore of reloading. This 'Foster mount' became standard on British Nieuports.

During the Battle of Verdun Maj Gen Hugh M. Trenchard took note of the emergence of specialized French *escadrilles de chasse* and German *Kampfeinsitzer Kommandos*, and began to introduce such units to the RFC. The first homogeneous single-seat unit in the RFC, No. 24 Sqn, entered combat in April 1916 with Aircraft Manufacturing Company DH 2 pushers.

The first unit (No. 60 Sqn) to use tractor-engined scouts began operations in June with two flights of deflector-equipped Morane-Saulnier Ns and one of Morane-Saulnier BB two-seater biplanes. After a calamitous time over the Somme with the 'Bullets' (including 110hp Morane-Saulnier Is and Vs) No. 60 Sqn was re-stocked with Nieuport 16s and 17s in October. As one consequence of the unit's poor experience with the 'Bullet', Nieuport sesquiplanes from 17 through to 27 would be part of the RFC's arsenal until the early spring of 1918. Another consequence was to leave Trenchard with a prejudice against monoplanes that would last for virtually the duration of the war.

LUFTSTREITKRÄFTE

Like their French counterparts, the first German fighter pilots emerged from an existing pool of reconnaissance and bomber aircrews. An experienced pilot with an already proven track record over the front had an obvious edge for selection, but aggressiveness was a plus, and there was no better demonstration of that than being credited with an aerial victory while on two-seater duty, as Ltn Oswald Boelcke was over a Morane-Saulnier L of MS15 on 4 July 1915.

To a greater degree than his French adversaries, however, the German pilot with dreams of becoming a Fokker *Eindecker Kanone* faced the added learning curve of familiarizing himself with an exotically different powerplant. Mastering the rotary engine required more attention on his part, as well as from his mechanic, than did the liquid-cooled inline engines that powered the vast majority of German aircraft. Although

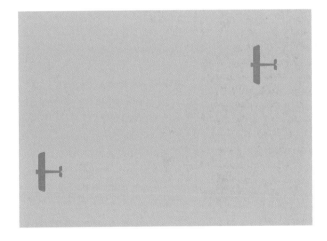

light, mechanically simple and offering a nimbler touch in the air, the rotary, with its spinning cylinders, produced more torque than the average German pilot was used to. Acceleration and deceleration also had to be handled differently, with the rotary engine requiring more finesse in the way it was operated. Finally, pilots had to get used to being constantly sprayed by lubricant thrown out by the rapidly spinning engine.

One would-be fighter pilot who learned this the hard way was Ltn Manfred *Freiherr* von Richthofen, who was flying Albatros C IIIs with *Kampfstaffel* 8 on the Verdun front in May 1916 when a Fokker E III was delivered to his unit. For a short time the fighter was shared between von Richthofen and Ltn d R Hans Reimann until, during a landing, the engine malfunctioned and the aeroplane crashed, ending von Richthofen's dreams of glory...at least for the time being.

Boelcke's early success in the Fokker E I could in large part be traced to previous experience acquired through good fortune. On 11 November 1914 Ltn Otto Parschau, then attached to the *Brieftauben-Abteilung*, or carrier pigeon section Ostende (whose designation masked its real purpose – to explore means of bombing England), landed his Fokker A III (M 5L) at Pontfaverger, near Reims, where Ltn Boelcke was then serving in FFA 13. The two

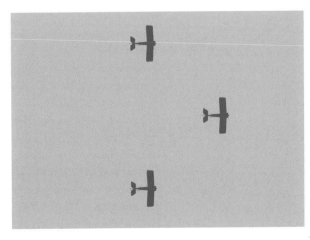

airmen had met earlier in Darmstadt, and soon Parschau had briefed the insatiably curious Boelcke on the differences between the Fokker, with its Oberursel A O engine, and the heavier biplane two-seaters he was used to. Upon taking it up Boelcke swiftly got the hang of the monoplane and its engine, and subsequently petitioned his superiors for a Fokker of his own, which was finally delivered on 9 December.

Boelcke thus had a valuable leg up on his future fighting career when Parschau and Anthony Fokker arrived at FFA 62 in the summer of 1915 to train him and his section mate, Ltn Max Immelmann, in the new E I. Their familiarity with rotary engines allowed them to devote more of their attention to flying and fighting, as well as devising tactics for using the new fighters.

Loath to let their secret weapon fall into Allied hands as Garros' deflectors had fallen into their own, the German High Command ordered the Fokkers to operate strictly on their side of the lines. Boelcke flagrantly disobeyed that order until he was nearly shot down by an Allied aeroplane while attacking another in enemy territory. That incident underscored for him the reason for the standing order not to cross the lines, while making it equally clear that lone wolf tactics would not suffice to achieve meaningful local air superiority.

Based on that epiphany, Boelcke envisioned patrols by two Fokkers, with a wingman flying slightly above and to the side to guard the leader's tail. In spite of the friendly rivalry that developed between them, Boelcke and Immelmann came to work quite successfully as a team. Indeed, their scores were tied at six when they both received the *Orden Pour le Mérite* on 12 January 1916.

By then too, the Fokker E I had been joined by some improved progeny – the somewhat enlarged E II, powered by a 100hp Oberursel U I engine, and the E III, whose increased fuel capacity raised its flight duration from 90 to 150 minutes.

By the end of October there were 75 Fokkers at the front, 23 of them E IIIs. Alotted to various units, the *Eindeckers* were flown with enthused élan to produce a new generation of German fighting heroes, such as Parschau, Hans Berr, Wilhelm Frankl, Walter Höhndorf, Gustav Leffers, Max Mulzer and Kurt Student.

In the following months, however, the appearance of Nieuport *Bébé* scouts, with their superior overall performance and growing numbers, asserted that the Fokker's half-year of ascendency was the product of its synchronized gun and the skill of the handful of pilots who flew it, rather than any outstanding characteristics of the aeroplane itself. Experienced hands such as Boelcke and Rudolf Berthold called for a new generation of stronger and more powerful biplanes to replace the *Eindeckers*.

In 1916 the grouping of Nieuport scouts in squadrons and, later, provisional combat groups swiftly marginalized the lone 'knight of the air'. Curiously, though, the Germans were neither quick nor consistent in responding to the French challenge. Throughout 1915 odd Fokkers assigned to *Feldflieger Abteilungen* had been detached in autonomous, provisional '*Kommandos*' that generally comprised one or two scouts. Initially FFA 23 at Vaux had a *Kommando* consisting of a Fokker and an AEG G II twin-engined *Kampfflugzeug*, both operating in a fighting capacity that allowed its most aggressive pilot, Oblt Rudolf Berthold, to evaluate both aeroplanes and conclude that the single-engined single-seater was hands down the better way to go. On 11 January 1916 his unit was officially designated *Eindecker Kommando* Vaux, at which point it had five Fokkers. Its formation set a standard for KEKs, which would in turn provide the nucleus of the more permanent *Jagdstaffeln* to come.

Perhaps the most significant development on the German side since the Fokker E I entered combat came from Oswald Boelcke before leaving the front at the end of June 1916. Taking careful stock of his experience over Verdun, he formulated and wrote up a list of tactics and strategies that would help his comrades-in-arms make the most of the aeroplanes they had, as well as the better ones to come – a '*Diktat*' that constituted the first fighter doctrine.

Few Fokker pilots achieved acedom in 1916, and a sizeable percentage of them did not survive to see 1917. Those who did acquired a wealth of experience that made them good fighter leaders as the state of the art advanced. One survivor was Kurt Student, who summarized his wartime exploits in a letter to William R. Puglisi of the American *Cross & Cockade Society* in 1960:

> My first single seater command was the 'Army *Fokkerstaffel*' that was formed on 1 June 1916 and assigned to the Third German Army. We had six Fokker 'E' type monoplanes, and our flying field was at Vousiers [sic]. From 1 July 1916 to May 1918 we were stationed at Leffincourt, in the Champagne area. In October 1916 my group became *Jagdstaffel* 9.
>
> My first victory was over a Nieuport 11 on 6 July 1916. The aircraft was captured intact, together with its pilot, Lt Rathi [sic], who was taken prisoner.

Born in Birkholtz, Brandenburg, in 1890 and commissioned in 1911, Oblt Student had had an unconfirmed success over a Russian Morane-Saulnier on 30 September 1915 while flying Albatros two-seaters with FFA 17 over the Galician Front. Typically, his feat led to his selection for training in *Eindeckers*. After bringing down Sous-Lt Jean Raty of

WALTER HÖHNDORF

Being among the relative handful of German Fokker aces whose scores included Nieuport *Bébés* was but one of many facets of Walter Höhndorf's aviation career. Born in Prutzke the son of a school teacher on 10 November 1892, Höhndorf was educated in West Brandenburg and Schöneberg. During this time he developed a fascination with motors and engineering mechanics that

Walter Höhndorf (Lance Bronnenkant)

Château-Salins on 17 June, was apparently a Nieuport two-seater of N68, which went down in French lines with its crew wounded. Höhndorf scored two more victories in the Toul sector before transferring to KEK Vaux at the end of June. On 15 July he was credited with downing Nieuport 16 N1392, killing MdL Georges Nautre of N62. He raised his tally to nine on 19 July

soon extended to aeroplanes. He undertook flight training in Paris in September 1913 and earned brevet No. 582 on 3 November. Höhndorf went on to national renown as one of the first Germans to perform complicated aerobatic manoeuvres, and in January 1914 he began working at the Union Flugzeugwerke at Teltow.

When war broke out Höhndorf volunteered for flying, and was accepted at *Etappen-Flugzeug-Park* 1 in Dusseldorf on 12 August 1914. Two months later he was awarded the Iron Cross, 2nd Class and promoted to Unteroffizier in October 1914. On 15 March 1915 he was commissioned a Leutnant der Reserve. Höhndorf initially test flew giant multi-engined Siemens-Schuckert R aeroplanes, but later in the year he was assigned to FFA 12. While flying *Eindeckers* with that unit he scored his first two victories, a Voisin of VB105 on 17 January 1916 and one from VB101 two days later.

Höhndorf subsequently served in FFA 67, but was attached to *Fokkerstaffel* Falkenhausen on 10 April when he shot down Nieuport 11 N653 of N68 (Sous-Lt Marcel Tibérghein was taken prisoner). His fifth victory, south of

and received the *Orden Pour le Mérite* the next day. Höhndorf's fourth Nieuport victory, scored south of Bapaume on the 21st, was probably Lt Marie Henri Dagonet of N37 who, in spite of grievous wounds, made it back to Allied lines. Dagonet was made a *Chevalier de la Légion d'Honneur* for this act of bravery, but died in hospital at Wiencourt l'Equipée on the 22nd.

On 23 August Höhndorf became a founding member of *Jagdstaffel* 1, with whom he downed a Caudron G 4 on 17 September for his 12th victory, before moving on to *Jasta* 4. He then returned to test pilot duties, as well as instructing at the fighter school at Valenciennes, before taking command of *Jasta* 14 on 15 August 1917. Höhndorf also helped the Allgemeine Elektrizitäts Gesellschaft design a new biplane fighter, and he was test flying the prototype, AEG D I 4400/17, at Ire-le-Sec, near Marville, when he suffered a fatal crash on 5 September. He was buried there. In addition to the 'Blue Max', Walter Höhndorf received the *Ritterkreuz mit Schwerten der Hohenzollern Hausordnung* and the Iron Cross 1st and 2nd Classes.

N38 at Péronne on 1 July (who was wounded and made a PoW), Student was credited with a Caudron of C4 on 1 August. Seven days later Student drove a two-seater Nieuport of N38 down in Allied lines. Its pilot, Lt Hubert de Fels, was unhurt, but his observer, Sous-Lt Emile Deviterne, was wounded. Nearby, however, one of Student's pilots, Ltn Bruno Berneis, was shot down in flames by Sous-Lt Marcel Burguin, who was flying another of N38's single-seat Nieuports.

Student went on to command *Jasta* 9 from 5 October 1916 to 14 March 1918, and he scored three more victories in Albatros scouts. He would subsequently attain the rank of Generaloberst in World War II, commanding German airborne forces in such spectacular operations as the assaults of Eben Emael and Crete. Student died in 1978.

COMBAT

The Battle of Verdun began on 21 February 1916 with scout pilots from both sides targeting the enemy's reconnaissance aeroplanes, as would be a logical first priority. The first French claim over a Fokker E type that day was by a Maurice Farman bomber crew of *escadrille* MF29. First blood between the rival fighters may have finally been drawn on 26 February, when Adj Jean Navarre, newly transferred from N12 to N67 at Vadelaincourt, was credited with a double victory. French records refer to two two-seaters brought down, one of which was intact, but this is contradicted by their identifying two pilots killed – Ltns Georg Heine and Alfons von Zeddelmann – and an observer (Oblt Heinrich Kempf) taken prisoner at Dieue-sur-Meuse. This suggests that the aeroplane Navarre drove down at Dieue was a two-seater of *Kampfstaffel* 4 of *Kagohl* 1, while his second victim, which crashed at Manheulles, was a Fokker E III assigned to that unit for escort duties.

Whatever the case, they brought Navarre's score to five, and references to him as an *'as'* set a standard that his colleagues would soon strive to attain and surpass – notwithstanding the fact that at that point Adolphe Pégoud, Eugène Gilbert and Georges Guynemer had already done so, with six, five and seven victories, respectively.

In spite of Navarre's morale-raising feat, the five French observation units covering the Verdun sector (C11, C13, C18, MF63 and MF71) were finding themselves hard pressed to carry out their missions. Reinforcements in the form of MF19, MF20, C27 and C53 were quickly transferred in, but losses in the first three weeks rose to four aeroplanes destroyed and another 15 returning

damaged, with crewmen dead or wounded. The overall effect of these casualties added up to the situation that led Gen Pétain to call Cmdt de Rose to his headquarters on 28 February and issue his order, *'De Rose, je suis aveugle! Balayez-moi le ciel!'*

Nieuports proliferated, and so did the mutual carnage among two-seaters, but the next positive claim over an *Eindecker*, on 8 March, was by a Farman crew of MF5. On the same day Asp Pierre Navarre (Jean's twin brother) of N69 forced an enemy aeroplane to land in German lines – a promising start that nevertheless did not qualify as a victory by French standards. In a second sortie, however, he was shot down over Verdun with three bullets in his arm, having probably become the first victim of Oblt Hans Berr, who was serving with a Fokker *Kommando* at Avillers.

After visiting his brother in hospital, Jean Navarre returned to the fray swearing revenge – which he achieved ten days later with a two-seater over Vigneville. Before that, one of his comrades at N67, Sous-Lt Jean Peretti, was credited with a Fokker in flames over Fort Douaumont on 11 March, although there are no German casualties that match the claim.

Meanwhile, the recently arrived Hptm Oswald Boelcke had judged the front to be too far away for him and his pilots to observe with their telescopes from Jametz. Therefore, he moved up to Sivry on 10 March, taking Ltn Werner Notzke, an Unteroffizier and 15 enlisted men with him, but leaving the rest of his Fokkers at Jametz. The next day he downed a Farman for his tenth victory. Coincidentally, Navarre was unwittingly emulating Boelcke when he obtained permission from his CO, Capt Henri Constant de Saint-Sauveur, to establish a small camouflaged airfield closer to the frontlines so that he too could respond more quickly to enemy air activity. In order to conceal the location of the secret base for as long as possible he would cut his engine and glide in for a landing at dusk. Eventually the Germans did cotton on, and they targeted the airstrip with their artillery. Navarre was forced to abandon it and return to Vadelaincourt.

On 12 March Ltn Parschau of *Kagohl* 1 was credited with a Nieuport in the Verdun area, Adj Auguste Metairie of N49 coming down wounded in French lines. The next day Boelcke, taking off from Sivry, reported seeing a German reconnaissance aeroplane

An officer believed to be Ltn Hans Berr of KEK Cunel peers from the cockpit of Fokker E III 420/15. Berr was credited with a Nieuport on 8 March 1916, which may well have been flown by Asp Pierre Navarre of N69, who came down in French lines badly wounded. (Lance Bronnenkant)

over Fort Douaumont beset by a French fighter, which he attacked and drove away. This presents the intriguing possibility of a chance encounter between two of the war's most illustrious names. During his second patrol that day the newly commissioned Sous-Lt Georges Guynemer – who had scored his eighth victory 24 hours earlier – was attacking an LVG head-on when a fusillade of enemy fire suddenly struck the cowling, wings and struts of his Nieuport 11 N836, also putting two bullets in his left arm and peppering his face with bullet fragments. After descending about 300 metres he recovered and landed at Borcourt. Hospitalized in Paris, Guynemer would not rejoin his *escadrille* until after N3's departure from the Verdun sector on 16 April.

In a letter to his comrade's parents that downplayed his wounds, noting that no bones had been touched, Lt Deullin wrote:

> The accident occurred this afternoon, at about four o'clock. Guynemer attacked a *Boche* and fired at him in his usual way. Another *Boche* about 200 metres away came to the rescue and fired a belt at an angle, of which you know the result. Guynemer was able to disengage easily and landed at our field.

Whether it was his or the LVG's forward-firing gun – or both – that may have terminated Guynemer's career over Verdun, Boelcke, having only seen his enemy disengage, made no claim, contenting himself with having aided the two-seater. There is, however, a time discrepancy against Deullin's placing Guynemer's wounding at 1600hrs, even allowing for German time being an hour ahead of the Allies'. Soon after his encounter over Douaumont, Boelcke attacked a French formation east of Malancourt at 1300hrs, and was credited with a 'Voisin' driven down just inside French lines for his 11th victory. The latter seems to have in fact been a Breguet-Michelin IV of BM118, whose crewmen were both wounded.

On 17 March Sgt Marcel Garet and Lt Jean Rimbaud of N23 were returning from a long reconnaissance in a Nieuport 10, escorted by two *Bébés* flown by Sgts Maxime Lenoir and Eduard Pulpe, when they spotted another French two-seater being attacked by several Fokkers. All three Nieuports hastened to its aid, but Garet and Rimbaud

Nieuport 11 N571, also decked out in blue, white and red on its fuselage and wheel hubs, served in N65 and was flown by American volunteer Cpl Elliott C. Cowdin before his transfer to N124. On 4 April 1916 Cowdin shot down an LVG for his only aerial success of the war, while squadronmate Adj Charles Nungesser scored his ace-making fifth victory over a 'two-engined' aeroplane on that same date. (SHDA B83-3506)

soon had to disengage when a Fokker wounded them both, only to be itself shot down near Dun-sur-Meuse by Lenoir and Pulpe. The Germans subsequently recorded the death of Ltn Horst von Gehe of *Kampfstaffel 26/Kagohl* 5 at Merci-le-Bas – far to the east of Dun, although it is possible that he may have been escorting his *Staffel's* two-seaters and succumbed to his wounds later that day.

In any case, the Fokker was the third victory for Lenoir and the first for Pulpe, a 34-year-old Latvian teacher from Riga who had been studying in France when war broke out and who had volunteered to serve in the *Aéronautique Militaire*. Rimbaud, one of whose arms had to be amputated, was subsequently made a *Chevalier de la Légion d'Honneur*, while Lenoir and Garet were awarded the *Médaille Militaire*.

Meanwhile, a 21 March directive from the German army headquarters declared the assigning of Fokkers in ones or twos to *Feldflieger Abteilungen* a failure as far as keeping Allied aircraft out of German airspace was concerned. As of 1 April, it declared, the fighters would be collected into two *Staffeln*:

> Airfield of the *West-Staffel* will be at Le Faux Ferme, northeast of Coucy. Airfield of the *Ost-Staffel* will be just west of St Erme. To *Fokker-Staffel-West* will go the aircraft of *Abteilungen* 7, 11 and 39 – four aeroplanes. To *Fokker-Staffel-Ost* will go the aircraft of *Abteilungen* 26 and 29 – five aeroplanes.

On 24 March Boelcke, who had been flying a Fokker E IV, wrote an extensive, far-from-glowing report on its performance:

> The machine loses much speed in climbing, so that several Nieuport biplanes escaped me in consequence. The climbing capacity falls off considerably at great heights (over 3,000m). This defect could be avoided by bringing out a light biplane. The manoeuvring power of the 160hp machine is considerably inferior to that of the 100hp and 80hp types because of the difficulty in countering the active force of the heavy engine.

Ltn d R Walter Höhndorf wryly reclines on 'standby alert' atop his Fokker E IV 437/15, which he flew with a fair amount of success with *Fokkerstaffel* Falkenhausen and KEK Vaux. His 12 victories included two Nieuports, but the second was probably a two-seater. (Greg VanWyngarden)

Given the greater numbers of Allied aircraft they faced, the Fokker pilots still had to take a defensive stance, but the formation of *Kampfeinsitzer Kommandos* did allow them to concentrate what they had towards more aggressively dealing with incursions into their airspace. *Idflieg* promised to address their technical concerns with a new generation of biplanes, but for the time being the *Eindecker* pilots would have to soldier on with that they had.

The vagaries of war were on display on 31 March when Nieuport 10 N454 of N12 was shot down near Laon by Uffz Hans Malz of FFA 39, flying one of the much-maligned Pfalz E Is – both crewmen perished. The outcome was reversed a few hours later when the crew of a two-seater from FFA 60 downed a Nieuport 11 from N57, killing its pilot, Sous-Lt Louis Beaujard. One of his *escadrille* mates, Lt André Dubois de Gennes, forced a Fokker to land in German lines, which was not credited to him, but so did Capt Joseph Vuillemin and the observer of his Caudron G 4 from C11. More definitively, Lt Deullin of N3, flying new Nieuport 16 N962, avenged Guynemer by sending a Fokker down to crash between Beaumont and Consenvoye, although its pilot apparently survived.

Rittm Erich *Graf* von Holck of FFA (A) 203 plays with his dog in front of his Fokker E III shortly before embarking on his last flight. (Greg VanWyngarden)

On 9 April Capt Louis Robert de Beauchamp, commander of N23, claimed his first victory in collaboration with Lt de Lage, a visiting pilot from *Groupe de Bombardement* 4, and the crew of the embattled Caudron of C42 they assisted, sending an attacking Fokker down to crash near Esnes. The Germans had mixed fortunes on the 10th. Lt d R Walter Höhndorf, flying a Fokker E IV with *Fokkerstaffel* Falkenhausen, brought Nieuport 11 N653 down for his third victory – its pilot, Sous-Lt Marcel Tiberghein of N68, was captured. The French, however, also obtained a valuable prize when E III 196/16 came down in their lines after Uffz Roessler of FFA 22 became disoriented and ran out of fuel. The French test flew the aeroplane and concluded that it was inferior to the Nieuport 11 in every respect except armament. A second E III similarly fell into French hands near Reims five days later.

Navarre claimed three Fokkers on 24 April, but none were confirmed. The next day Sous-Lt Jean Robert of N57 was credited with an *Eindecker* crashed near Hattonchâtel. Four days later the French reported a Fokker shooting down and mortally wounding Sous-Lt Jean Peretti, who had recently transferred from N3 to N67, after which a two-seater Nieuport 12 of N67, crewed by Sgt Robert de Marolles and Brig Léon Vitalis, sent Peretti's assailant crashing south of Hill 304, some 200m from the trenches. Curiously, there is neither a corresponding claim nor loss recorded among the Fokker units for that day.

The Germans lost three Fokker pilots on 30 April. Ltn Otto Schmedes of KEK Bertincourt was killed near Combles, having possibly fallen victim to N3's Sous-Lt Charles de Guibert, flying Nieuport 11 N917 – he had claimed two Fokkers destroyed over nearby Carrepuis and Roye. A third Fokker claim had also been made in the same area by 2Lt David M. Tidmarsh of No. 24 Sqn, who was flying a DH 2 at the time.

The second Fokker pilot killed on the 30th was downed by a Nieuport 16. Rittm Erich *Graf* von Holck of FFA (A) 203 had previously served in FFA 69 on the Eastern Front, where one of his observers had been Ltn Manfred *Freiherr* von Richthofen. Both were pilots serving over Verdun when von Richthofen, now flying an Albatros C III, witnessed Holck being shot down by Lt Deullin of N3 over Courriers Wood near Douaumont at 1100hrs – Deullin's fourth overall victory and his second Fokker.

The third German *Eindecker* pilot fell at 1745hrs after a bombing attack had drawn Sgt Jean Chaput of N31 skyward in pursuit. As the Frenchman crossed the lines he spotted 'a superb Fokker' above him at an altitude of 3,800m, with another following 500m behind it. Chaput attacked the first, but his gun jammed after one shot. As he pursued his diving quarry he had to rectify three more jams in quick succession before he got off three more shots. His weapon then jammed once more, but by then one round had struck home. The Fokker crashed in the Bois d'Eparges, its demise corresponding with German reports confirming the death of 39-year-old Vfw Erich Kügler of FFA 70 at Remy-la-Calonne.

'During this time his powerless little comrade, 500m behind me, frantically fired off his belt of explosive bullets at me', Chaput added. 'A rapid climb got rid of him, after which I descended again.' Kügler was his third victim of an eventual 16 before Chaput was himself mortally wounded in action on 6 May 1918.

A recent addition to Boelcke's flight at Sivry, Ltn Friedrich Mallinkrodt, claimed a French aeroplane over Verdun on 30 April. Although it was not confirmed, the French recorded MdL Paul Suisse of N37 coming down badly wounded in Allied lines. He succumbed to his injuries the next day.

The next two French Fokker claims for May came from Farman crews on the 4th and 10th. On the latter date a patrol of N69 Nieuports led by Capt Robert Massenet-Royer

The remains of Holck's aeroplane after his encounter with *escadrille* N3 on 30 April 1916, in which the former pilot and close friend of future 'Red Baron' Ltn Manfred *Frhr* von Richthofen was killed by Lt Albert Deullin – with von Richthofen bearing witness. (Aaron Weaver)

de Marancour forced a Fokker to land at Maucourt, but it was not credited. On 11 May the *escadrilles de chasse* lost their founding mastermind. Having turned down offers of a bomber command or a joint fighter and bomber command, Cmdt de Rose had convinced the military authorities that an independent French fighter arm should have a free hand to pre-emptively seize control of the air over critical areas of the front, taking on defensive or escort roles as secondary options when needed. Upon his return to the Verdun sector, he was performing a demonstration flight for the *Ve Armée's* new quartermaster general when his Nieuport 11 suddenly crashed.

It was an ironic death for an officer who had often criticized Jean Navarre for the unnecessary risks he took with his aerial stunting – and a terrible loss to the *Aéronautique Militaire*. But de Rose's disciples, starting with his successor, Capt Auguste le Révérend, would continue what he started, expanding the fighter force within larger and larger organizations in the next two years. As it was, his provisional groups had at least stalemated the *Eindeckers* above Verdun, as Nieuports and Morane-Saulniers, flying in flights of six or more, countered the advantages of the Fokkers' interrupter gear.

On 12 May Sous-Lt Georges Pelletier-Doisy of N12, in concert with Cmdt Paul du Peuty and Lt Henri de Chivre of N69, sent a Fokker crashing near Vaux. FFA 70 reported Ltn d R Hans Protz killed in an *Eindecker* at Charleville, but that he had perished in a flying accident.

The German fighters came out second best during two encounters on 17 May, starting with a Fokker sent crashing near Bezonvaux by Pelletier-Doisy. Elsewhere, Lt Jules de Boutigny of N23 was reconnoitring over Conflans and Longuyon when he was engaged by two *Eindeckers*, but he managed to force one down near Mangiennes.

ATTACK ON THE BALLOON LINE

A rare occasion when fighters found themselves in direct confrontation during the Verdun campaign occurred on 21–22 May, when Gen Robert Nivelle and his *IIe Armée* staff laid plans to retake Fort Douaumont. The counterattack was scheduled for the 22nd, and Capt le Révérend's *Groupe des Escadrilles de Chasse* was tasked with attacking any German reconnaissance aeroplanes that ventured over or near the frontlines. At the same time, volunteers were requested to eliminate eight German kite balloons

Oblt Boelcke's advance field at Sivry opened for business in March 1916. In this photograph Boelcke is apparently seated beside his Fokker E IV 123/15 (the second prototype) closest to the camera, while his wingman, Ltn Werner Notzke, is seated alongside his E IV. Notzke was killed on 21 April when the wing of his machine caught a balloon cable while he was practicing his shooting against a ground target. (Lance Bronnenkant)

ENGAGING THE ENEMY

Sighting the Fokker E I's machine gun was a simple matter of pointing the aeroplane at the target and taking aim via a pylon backsight and usually a rectangular 'gate' type foresight, both offset to port. The British, who evaluated captured Fokker E III 210/16, described it as having a rectangular foresight with two beads 43mm on either side of the centre, and a pylon backsight 920mm aft. Ring foresights also appeared on Fokkers, but less commonly.

The Nieuport's sights were similar in principle but less simple in execution, with a ring and pylon or a tube sight suspended from below the upper wing. Several seem to have been improvised, such as the forward ring sight braced by extra wires to the forward cabane struts just visible on Jean Chaput's Nieuport 16 N940 of N31. Some Nieuports had a somewhat elaborate platform ahead of the pilot, and a second set forward on a pedestal just aft of the engine cowling. All had to be carefully adjusted to accommodate the Lewis gun.

Jamming was a problem on both sides. In the Fokker's case, the pilot could reach forward to rectify the jam and hope that it had not thrown the interrupter gear out of synchronization. The Nieuport pilot had no synchronization issues to worry about, but a jammed gun had to be pulled down, cleared and returned to the firing position, all in the face of his own propwash.

Two days after his encounter with two Fokkers on 30 April 1916, Chaput wrote, 'I attacked the first, and at a distance of ten metres I fired – the machine gun loosed off one shot and jammed. The surprised Fokker went into a descent and I accompanied him while struggling with my machine gun, which, shot after shot, jammed twice without firing at all – finally it fired three bullets in a row. Without a doubt they were well adjusted, for the monoplane began a fabulous descent and, guided by the wind, crashed in the ravine "without a name" [Éparges Wood]'.

A rare colour photograph of Sgt Jean Chaput of N31 beside his Nieuport 16 N940 after he had downed a Fokker on 30 April 1916. N962, flown by N3's Lt Albert Deullin that same day, would have looked similar to this machine – N3's soon to be famous stork insignia did not start appearing on the unit's aircraft until June. (Private Collection)

lined up along the target area north of the Meuse River. Eight pilots duly gathered at Lemmes – *Capt* Louis Robert de Beauchamp and Lt Jules de Boutigny of N23, Sous-Lt Jean Chaput of N31, Lt André Dubois de Gennes and Adj Lucien Barrault of N57, Sous-Lt Charles Nungesser and Adj Henri Réservat of N65, and Sgt Joseph Henri Guiguet, a member of *escadrille* N95 of the *Camp Retranché de Paris* who had been testing the new Le Prieur rockets.

On 21 May N65's Capt Philippe Féquant, with two escorts, reconnoitred the right bank of the Meuse to locate the enemy balloon nests. Frontline German observers reported their presence to Jametz and soon one of Féquant's wingmen, Adj Henri Brion, came under attack from three enemy aeroplanes. He returned wounded, his Nieuport badly damaged. Meanwhile, Sgt Georges Kirsch was also jumped by two German scouts, which put three bullets in him and riddled his aeroplane before he disengaged and force landed in French lines. Both Nieuports were credited to Hptm Boelcke as his 17th and 18th victories, which he reported sending down south of Mort Homme and the Bois de Hesse, respectively. In spite of the loss of his escorts, Féquant brought back the necessary intelligence.

On the 22nd the eight fighters set out as planned. N65 had a fruitful day, with Féquant claiming an LVG over Beaumont and Adj Michel Le Roy downing an Aviatik at Flabas. Over Gincrey Nungesser destroyed a *Drachen*, and though Barrault, who accompanied them, missed a second 'gasbag' with his rockets, one of the four that Réservat fired sent it down in flames.

Adj Charles Nungesser of N 65 faces the camera near the rudder of his Nieuport 16 N880 at Lemmes shortly before eight Nieuports depart on the mission to eliminate German balloons along the Meuse River on 22 May. In spite of Fokker opposition, the attackers succeeded in destroying six of their eight targets. (Greg VanWyngarden)

As the balloon raiders headed for home Nungesser and Réservat were intercepted by German fighters near Étain. Nungesser scattered his adversaries and returned, but Réservat's Nieuport 16 N959 was hit by ground fire and forced to land with four rockets still in their tubes. These were closely studied by his German captors. Réservat later escaped on 19 March 1917 and made his way back to France.

Guiguet's target at Sivry was strategically located on hills that provided an unobstructed view of the valley and both sides of the river – and, not coincidentally, was home to Boelcke's fighter flight. Diving to an altitude of 1,000m, Guiguet fired off all eight 'aerial torpedoes' and saw one strike home. The resulting explosion killed the balloon's observer, Oblt Friedrich von Zanthier, and threw Guiguet's Nieuport 16, N978, into a spin, but he recovered and regained Allied lines with several Fokkers in hot pursuit.

Elsewhere along the line, de Beauchamp destroyed his *Drachen* east of Flabas, but de Boutigny's firing system failed. Chaput and de Gennes burned their targets north-west and north-east of Ornes, respectively.

A few hours after the attack, the 36e, 54e, 74e and 129e *Régiments d'Infanterie* assaulted Fort Douaumont, but were stopped short of their objective. This was no fault of the Nieuport pilots, who in eliminating six of the targeted eight balloons had fulfilled their mission admirably, but rather several days of French artillery barrage that was meant to 'soften up' the objective but only served to alert the Germans, who stiffened their defences.

The next encounter between *Bébé* and *Eindecker* occurred on 24 May when newly promoted Lt William Thaw, leading N124's first morning patrol, surprised a Fokker E III and brought it down north of Vaux. Thaw's French commander, Capt Georges Thenault, was leading a second sortie when it encountered 12 German aircraft over Etain. Without waiting for Thenault's attack signal, an overeager Cpl Victor Chapman promptly dived at the enemy, followed by Cpl Kiffin Rockwell and Thaw.

In the ensuing melee Chapman claimed a Fokker OOC, although he was wounded in the arm. Rockwell's windscreen was hit and his face lacerated by glass and bullet fragments, but he too claimed a victory before returning to Behonne. Thaw claimed a third Fokker before his Lewis gun jammed. As he turned back, he was fired upon by two Aviatiks, one of which put bullets through his fuel tank and left elbow, breaking his arm. Gliding over the lines, Thaw pancaked near Fort Travennes, was taken to the hospital at Neuilly and subsequently convalesced at his sister's residence in Paris. Only Thaw's earlier Fokker was credited, this being his first victory of an eventual five.

MORE *BÉBÉ* ADOPTIONS

The first Fokker E I appeared over Flanders in September 1915 when Flgobmt Erich Bödecker began escorting naval two-seaters on their reconnaissance sorties. This was in response to the appearance of the first Belgian scout, a single-seat Nieuport 10 flown by Lt Henri Crombez, on 26 August. Although an able and dedicated aviator, Crombez lacked a fighter pilot's temperament. However, the third Belgian assigned a modified Nieuport 10, pre-war motorcycle champion and aerobat Sgt Jan Olieslagers, did. On 12 September he sent an Aviatik crashing in enemy lines for Belgium's first single-seater victory.

The Fokker's presence in Flanders, relatively modest though it was, did not go unnoticed by the British. Even while the French were marshalling their *Bébés* for introduction in *escadrille* strength, the RNAS began assigning its Nieuport 11s to 'squadrons' within its squadron-sized wings almost two months before the first one arrived at N31 in January 1916. Their presence along the Flanders coast led the *Kriegsmarine* to acquire more Fokker E IIIs and create fighter detachments for them, starting in April 1916 with a *Kampfeinsitzer Kommando* within *Marine Feldflieger Abteilung* I at Mariakerke, led by Ltn z S Gotthard Sachsenberg, and a second KEK assigned to MFFA II at Neumünster.

Fokker E III LF 196 was accepted by the German army on 28 March 1915 and then transferred to the navy on 9 April, which operated it until 30 November when it was written off. Amongst those to fly the aeroplane was Lt z S Gotthard Sachsenberg, who would later command the first *Marine Feld Jagdstaffel*. (Greg VanWyngarden)

MARK POSTLETHWAITE .13

While the French were massing their Nieuport fighters over Verdun, the RFC prepared to support its Somme offensive with Nos. 24, 29 and 32 Sqns, equipped with DH 2 pushers. The RFC had also acquired a handful of Nieuport 16s, but those were allotted to reconnaissance squadrons. A notable example was No. 11 Sqn, whose FE 2bs had an escort flight of three Nieuports, one of whose pilots was Lt Albert Ball.

On 29 May 1916 Ball flew scout 5173 (one of nine 16s purchased directly from Nieuport) on a lone sortie in which he engaged four Fokkers and an LVG, driving down the latter in a vertical dive and chasing off the *Eindeckers*. Later that day he was credited with an Albatros 'forced to land'. In the action depicted in this artwork, which took place on 1 June 1916, Ball flew Nieuport 5173 over to Douai – home of Oblt Max Immelmann's KEK, among others – and circled above the aerodrome for the next 30 minutes until an Albatros and a Fokker finally rose to his challenge. The two-seater attacked first, but after Ball fired ten rounds at it the Albatros pilot dived away and returned to the aerodrome. At that point the Fokker got on Ball's tail, closed the range and opened fire. The moment it did Ball, who had been waiting for that all along, whipped his Nieuport around and returned fire. The Fokker then turned away, dived and alit in a field two miles from the aerodrome.

Ball was credited with the Fokker as 'forced to land' for his fourth victory. He would score his fifth by burning a kite balloon on the 25th, thus becoming only the third British pilot to achieve that milestone.

Encounters between the fighters were rare, but on 8 July Flt Lt Thomas F. N. Gerrard, in Nieuport 3989 of 2 Naval Flight, 'A' Naval Squadron, 1 Naval Wing, operating from Furnes, drove a Fokker down OOC two miles from Ostend. The next day Stanley Dallas, in Nieuport 3994, claimed another E type OOC near Mariakerke. After their unit evolved into 1 Naval Squadron RNAS, 'Teddy' Gerrard would add eight more victories to his tally in Sopwith Triplanes in 1917, and a tenth victory in a Sopwith Camel in April 1918. Dallas' total had risen to at least 32 by the time he was killed in action in an SE 5a of No. 40 Sqn, Royal Air Force, on 1 June 1918. By then the German naval fighter units had also expanded, starting with the amalgamation of MFFA I and II's KEKs into *Marine Feld Jasta* I, under Sachsenberg's command, on 1 February 1917.

While the French massed their fighters over Verdun, the RFC likewise fielded its first single-seat fighter unit, No. 24 Sqn with DH 2s, at Bertangles in preparation for the offensive along the Somme River scheduled for 1 July. Although it had balked at purchasing Nieuport 11s from the French, the RFC acquired a handful of Nieuport 16s, which it allotted to reconnaissance squadrons. One such unit was No. 11 Sqn, which after replacing its Vickers FB 5s with FE 2bs also had an escort of Bristol Scouts, flown, among others, by 18-year-old Lt Albert Ball.

Transferred from No. 13 to No. 11 Sqn on 7 May, Ball was flying Bristol 5312 (fitted with interrupter gear designed by Vickers employees Harold Savage and George Henry Challenger) nine days later when he drove an Albatros C III of *Kampfstaffel* 17 down in German lines. The Vickers-Challenger gear's connecting rod proved too long and flexible to be reliable, however, and shortly after Ball's exploit No. 11 Sqn obtained three Nieuport 16s to supplement the Bristols.

Tricky though the Nieuport 16 was to fly, Ball took to it quickly enough to engage in three inconclusive combats on 22 May. Although he damaged A126's lower right wingtip in a bad landing on the 27th, during the course of the next month he mastered Nieuport 5173 sufficiently enough to use it effectively in combat. His first encounter with the enemy in the new aircraft came on 29 May, as he described in a combat report that revealed his trademark aggressiveness:

I had four fights in one patrol in my Nieuport, and came off top in every fight. Four Fokkers and an LVG attacked me about 12 miles over the lines. I forced the LVG down with a drum-and-a-half, after which I zoomed up after the Fokkers. They ran away at once. Out of all the fights I only got about eight shots into my machine, one of which just missed my back and hit the strut. However, on my way home, the Hun 'Archie' guns hit the tail of my machine and took a piece away, but I got back and have now got a new tail. The other fights were with Albatros machines.

Ball was credited with an LVG last seen in a vertical dive, counted as OOC, and another forced to land. The next day he flew the repaired 5173 over to Douai aerodrome – home of Oblt Max Immelmann's KEK, among others – and spent 30 minutes circling at 10,000ft before two enemy aeroplanes (an Albatros and a Fokker) finally took off. The two-seater attacked first, but after Ball fired ten rounds at it, its pilot dived away and returned to the aerodrome. At that point the Fokker came up from behind, but the moment it fired, Ball, who had been aware of its presence all along, whipped his Nieuport around and returned fire. The Fokker turned away, dived and alit in a field two miles from the aerodrome – a 'forced landing' that was credited as another victory for Ball.

A balloon burned on 25 June brought his official tally, tenuous as some of it might have been, to five. Ball had become the third British pilot to 'make ace', although the RFC was prone to discourage the sort of cult status that that distinction was coming to attain among the French and Germans.

By that time the reorganized Belgian air arm had acquired some Nieuport 11s, which were assigned to the 1e *Escadrille* to escort reconnaissance aeroplanes of that and other units. One of its members was recently promoted Sous-Lt Jan Olieslagers, who marked the cowling of his *Bébé* with his pre-war nickname 'Le Démon'. On 17 June he was escorting Farman F 40 2265 of the 4e *Escadrille*, crewed by Adj Charles Kervyn de Lettonhove and Capt Roger Lesergent d'Hendecourt, when he saw his charge come under attack by a Fokker E III over Poelkapelle at 1515hrs. The Farman crew drove down that assailant OOC, only to be shot up by another *Eindecker*, but by then Olieslagers had reached them and he despatched the Fokker. His adversary, credited as his second victory of an eventual six, was apparently Gfr Alfred Jäkel of FFA 221, who died of his wounds three days later.

Sgt Jan Olieslagers of the Belgian 1e *Escadrille de Chasse* beside his Nieuport 11, which boasted a fuselage roundel and the pilot's pre-war nickname *Le Démon* applied to the upper cowling. Having scored his first victory in a Nieuport 10, Olieslagers downed his second (a Fokker E III) while aiding a Farman F 40 on 18 June 1916. (Collection de Burlet via Walter Pieters)

Olieslagers was not the only one for whom 17 June proved to be memorable. Sgt Victor Chapman of N124 was on a lone foray that day when he spotted two enemy reconnaissance aeroplanes, one of which he forced to land near Béthincourt, although he had no witnesses to confirm it. He was then jumped by the two-seaters' three Fokker escorts, whose fire severed his Nieuport's right aileron control rod and creased his skull. Grabbing the ends of the control rods and gripping the control column with his knees, Chapman managed to land at Froidos aerodrome.

On that same morning Sous-Lts Jean Navarre and Gaston Guignand of N67 were patrolling with Navarre's friend Sous-Lt Pelletier-Doisy of N69 when they encountered a two-seater over Samogneux, which Navarre and Pelletier-Doisy shot down at 0600hrs. Continuing their sortie, they came upon another German aeroplane directing artillery fire over Grandpré, but as they were manoeuvring into position to attack, Navarre was suddenly shot through the right arm and chest. Spinning down, with his comrades diving after him, Navarre recovered sufficiently to land at an airfield near St Menehould. From there he was rushed to hospital at Chanzy. This ended the fighting career of the 'Sentinel of Verdun', whose score then stood at 12.

It has been suggested that Chapman or Navarre may have been victims of Walter Höhndorf, then operating with KEK Vaux and credited with a Nieuport in French

A Nieuport 16 flown by Sgt Georges de Geuser of N37 sallies forth over the Verdun front. After sharing in bringing down an Aviatik of Bavarian FFA 102 with Sgt Fernand Garrigou on 29 July 1916, de Geuser went missing on 17 September. (SHDA B89.4988)

lines near Château-Salins that same day. Neither pilot was wounded anywhere near Château-Salins, however, Höhndorf's victim more likely being a Nieuport 10 of N68 in a fight during which Sgt Jules Vigouroux and Sous-Lt Théophile Burgué were credited with a Fokker that crashed east of Bezanges, but Sgts Joseph Borde and Blain were driven down wounded in French lines.

Kiffin Rockwell believed that Chapman had been wounded by Boelcke, which is possible given their close proximity in the sector. Moreover, Boelcke described a fight with six of the 'Americans' that he'd heard about and had sought out 'to say how-do-you-do', during which he got behind 'a fairly raw beginner' and at a distance of about 100m 'sat on his neck and started work on him'. At that point, however, Boelcke reported one of his E IV's guns jamming after 20 rounds and the other after 50, forcing him to sideslip and dive to an altitude of about 800m so as to escape the other five Nieuports that followed him down. Under the circumstances it is not surprising that he claimed no success in the action.

Of eight Fokkers claimed by the French between late May and the end of June, only one was credited to a single-seater, when Sous-Lt Gaetan de la Brunetière of N68 drove one down after a hard fought engagement over the Forêt de Bézange on 30 June. His probable victim, Ltn Leopold Reimann of FFA 32, crash-landed in German lines in Fokker E III 347/15, shaken but unharmed, while de la Brunetière was wounded.

On 1 July the British Somme offensive became the main focus of activity on and over the Western Front, even though the Battle of Verdun would rage on to the end of the year. The Nieuport 11 and 16 *Bébés* had virtually ended the 'Fokker Scourge' there, but by June they were being rapidly replaced by the improved Nieuport 17. On the German side, eight Halberstadt biplanes had reached the front by the end of June, to be joined by Fokker biplanes such as the D I, D II and D III. Each of these transitional designs had its limitations, but in late August two new biplane fighters began to reach the front that would dramatically alter the tempo and very nature of the air war – the SPAD VII and the Albatros D II.

STATISTICS AND ANALYSIS

The struggle for Verdun – more of a campaign than a battle per se – saw the first use of massed air assets and for several months pitted a frail German monoplane with a highly effective weapon system against a French design of somewhat superior structure and performance, armed with a makeshift, rather awkward gun mounting suspended above the pilot's head. Their confrontation more often took the form of attacking one another's two-seater reconnaissance aeroplanes than each other – as well it should, since 'blinding' the enemy was very much their primary purpose. Their actual encounters were relatively infrequent, yet sufficient to convince the Germans that the Fokker monoplane's fortunes were on the wane.

In analysing the instances of when *Bébé* met *Eindecker* one must keep in mind that this was the first clash of its kind, and the antagonists were learning the finer points of their deadly art as they went. Their task was simply to drive the enemy from the sky by attacking whatever aeroplane they encountered. This fact is reflected in a survey of French claims over 'Fokkers' and 'scouts' during the Nieuport *Bébé*'s time as the principal French fighter – roughly between February and June 1916. According to French aviation historian David Méchin, the *Aéronautique Militaire* claimed a total of 74 German aircraft in aerial combat between 21 February and 1 July 1916 (when the British launched their Somme offensive), but most of its claims were over LVG two-seaters. During the same time period German pilots made 37 aerial claims, of which 27 were credited to aviators flying *Eindeckers*. Only six of their claims were over Nieuport single-seaters, however.

Nieuport 11 N1222 was flown by Sous-Lt Raymond Lis of N15 from Lemmes between 6 and 13 April 1916. Although his task was to keep the sky clear for reconnaissance aeroplanes like the Caudron G 4 in the background, the latter often faced the Fokkers on their own – and were credited with almost as many of them shot down as the Nieuports. (SHDA B81-26)

The author's own examination of French claims during that five-month period identified 12 Fokkers being credited to Nieuport 11 or 16 pilots, along with one shared with a Nieuport 10 crew. Two others were credited exclusively to Nieuport 10s. In that same time period, however, another 11 Fokkers were credited to Caudron G 4 crews and 12 to Maurice Farman crews. On the face of it, one might infer that the two-seaters were not all that helpless, and the single-seat Nieuports not quite so decisive a factor in breaking the 'Fokker Scourge' as posterity has been led to believe.

Hard numbers are not necessarily the whole story when the human factor is taken into account. A comment by Ltn Rudolf Berthold, translated by German aviation expert Peter M. Grosz, reveals a professional assessment of the Nieuport's impact on German fighter operations in the midsummer of 1916:

We had too few qualified monoplanes. We lacked an aircraft that was easily manoeuvrable in combat. We had fallen asleep on the laurel wreaths that the single-seaters in the hands of a few superlative pilots had achieved. It was not the monoplane itself, but the pilots who were responsible for the success. One need but compare the number of Fokker fighters at the Front with those few pilots who had victories. I had already requested a new type of aircraft in January 1916 – a small biplane. People laughed! The Frenchman meanwhile takes our experience to heart, quietly builds small biplanes and

Whatever its inherent advantages over the Fokker *Eindecker*, the Nieuport 11 could still fall victim to a skilled, canny opponent. Such a fate befell N653 flown by Sous-Lt Marcel Tiberghein of N68, who was forced down in German lines on 10 April 1916 by Ltn Walter Höhndorf, then flying an E IV with *Fokkerstaffel* Falkenhausen. (Greg VanWyngarden)

then launches hundreds at once against our lines. He has achieved air superiority and, with grinding teeth, we must watch while he shoots down our monoplanes and we're helpless.

Actions could speak louder than words. On 1 July 1916 Oblt Kurt Student, commanding *Armee-Oberkommando 3*'s *Fokkerstaffel* at Leffincourt, showed his skill with the Fokker E IV when he brought Nieuport 11 N1324 down intact behind German lines, where its wounded pilot, Sous-Lt Jean Raty of N38, was taken prisoner. After evaluating his prize Student judged the Nieuport's flight characteristics to be so much better than his own aeroplane's that he installed an LMG 08 with interrupter gear on it, repainted it in German markings, complete with a personal motif of crossed fencing swords, and flew combat missions in it.

The ultimate endorsement. After managing to bring down Nieuport 11 N1324 intact on 1 July 1916, Oblt Kurt Student had a synchronized LMG 08 machine gun installed and the French markings overpainted in a light colour with a crossed swords fuselage motif. He then used the Nieuport to supplement his Fokker E IV at Leffincourt. (Greg VanWyngarden)

Student was not alone. In September 1916, at a time when newly formed *Jagdstaffel* 1 at Bertincourt was operating a maddeningly mixed bag of Fokker monoplane and biplane scouts, as well as Halberstadt biplanes – while *Jasta* 2 was fully equipped with game-changing Albatros D Is and D IIs – Ltn d R Gustav Leffers often flew a captured Nieuport 16. Like Student, he too had installed a synchronized machine gun and repainted the French scout with Maltese crosses.

Leading Nieuport 11 and 16 Fokker *Eindecker* killers		
Pilot	Fokkers	Total
Albert Deullin	2	20
Maxime Lenoir	2	11
Georges Pelletier d'Oisy	2	6
Albert Ball	1	44
Jean Chaput	1	16
Roderic Stanley Dallas	1	32
Thomas F. N. Gerrard	1	10
Jean Navarre	1	12
Jan Olieslagers	1	6
William Thaw	1	5

Leading Fokker *Eindecker* Nieuport 11 and 16 killers		
Pilot	Nieuports	Total
Oswald Boelcke	3	40
Walter Höhndorf	3	12
Otto Parschau	1	8
Kurt Wintgens	1	16
Kurt Student	1	6

AFTERMATH

Since the summer of 1915 Germany's first single-seat fighters, the Fokker E I, E II and E III, had dominated the airspace over the Western Front – not because of their outstanding performance so much as that they were armed with a synchronized machine gun. The 'Fokker Scourge' could only go on so long, however, before the

A transitionary collection of Nieuport 11s, 16s, 17s and 21s line up at N103's aerodrome at Cachy in September 1916. (SHDA B96-1285)

Allies found ways to counter it, ranging from pusher scouts, such as the British DH 2, to better performing tractor fighters with machine guns mounted above the upper wing to fire over the propeller, such as the French Nieuport 11 and 16. Finally, fighters with interrupter gear of their own, such as the British Sopwith Scout (better known as the 'Pup') and the French Nieuport 17 and SPAD VII were introduced.

By the time the Battle of the Somme commenced on 1 July 1916, Allied fighters had virtually retaken control of the sky. Maj Wilhelm Siegert, commander of the *Idflieg*, wrote in outspoken retrospect:

> The start of the Somme battle unfortunately coincided with the low point in the technical development of our aircraft. The unquestioned supremacy we had enjoyed in early 1916 by virtue of our Fokker monoplane fighters shifted over to the enemy's Nieuport, Vickers [a German misidentification of the DH 2] and Sopwith aircraft in March and April. Our monthly aircraft output did not even allow a squadron to be equipped with a common type. For example, *Flieger Abteilung* 23 had a complement of five different aircraft types.

By October 1916 the aerial balance of power had begun to shift again. In large part Siegert attributed the German resurgence to the 'enterprise of Boelcke and his "school" in conjunction with the new Halberstadt D III fighter'. That was not exactly true. Granted, the Halberstadt biplanes, most notably the D II, proved to be less fragile and

Ltn Kurt Wintgens boards the Fokker E IV that he brought to *Jagdstaffel* 1. While the Halberstadt D II in the background was structurally sounder, it only carried one machine gun. Clinging to the twin-gunned *Eindecker* proved Wintgens' undoing on 25 September 1916, when he fell victim to Lt Alfred Heurteaux of N3, who was flying a SPAD VII. (Greg VanWyngarden)

have better overall performance than Fokker's *Eindeckers* or the D I, D II, D III and D IV biplanes intended to replace them.

The importance of the Halberstadt, however, was more transitionary in nature, for it helped to establish the biplane as structurally sounder than the monoplane and duly became an early mainstay of the new, specialized fighter squadrons, or *Jagdstaffeln*, which began to form in August 1916. The first of these was *Jasta* 1, organized from *Abwehr Kommando Nord* under the command of Hptm Martin Zander on the 22nd, followed by *Jasta* 2, under Hptm Oswald Boelcke, five days later. Both units started out with Fokker D Is and D IIs, but on 16 September *Jasta* 2 received the forerunner of a far more significant line of fighters, the Albatros D I.

One incident signalling the generational change in aerial warfare occurred on 25 September. Boelcke's *Jasta* 2 and its Albatrosen were hitting their stride, but *Jasta* 1 was still operating a mixed bag of old and new types. Indeed, Ltn Kurt Wintgens, now with at least 18 victories to his name, was still flying his veteran Fokker E IV, apparently because, for all its structural and performance advantages, the Halberstadt could only carry one machine gun and Wintgens preferred the E IV's double firepower.

So it was that while Wintgens was flying with Ltn Höhndorf over Villers-Carbonnel, they were ambushed at 1100hrs (1000hrs Allied time) and Höhndorf returned to report sadly that Wintgens' aeroplane had broken up under the enemy's fire. He had fallen victim to Lt Alfred Heurteaux of N3, flying in one of that unit's new SPAD VIIs – a fighter that was essentially two generations ahead of the *Eindecker*.

While the Fokkers were virtually gone from the Western Front by 1917, Gustave Delage's sesquiplane fighters soldiered on. The Nieuport 11 and 16 were swiftly replaced by the 17, although Macchi-built 11s continued to serve with considerable success in Italian *squadriglie*, as well as with Russian and Rumanian units on the Eastern Front. Nieuport, meanwhile, continued refining the formula with a succession of improved models – the 17bis, the 23, 24, 24bis and the 27 – which served alongside the SPADs in numerous French *escadrilles* and British squadrons.

The Germans, too, had been so impressed by the Nieuports' performance over Verdun and the Somme that *Idflieg* urged virtually every German fighter-producing firm to try adapting the sesquiplane formula to its own products. Superficially, the most blatant Nieuport copy to achieve limited manufacture was the Siemens-Schuckert D I. Arguably the most successful was the Albatros D III, which was essentially a late-model D II with its biplane wings replaced by a sesquiplane arrangement that sought to endow it with the best of both worlds – a fast, robust twin-gun fighter with improved cockpit visibility and manoeuvrability. That proved to be a tenuous balancing act on an airframe as heavy as the D III, which was fitted with a powerful engine. However, with extra bracing wires added it was just successful enough in skilled hands to make April 1917 a bloody month for the Allies.

The D III's more streamlined and 'lightened' successor, the D V, would be another story. Its debut in May 1917 was attended by an epidemic of wing failures that

handicapped its pilot's ability to fight, and necessitated so much beefing up that only the development of a higher compression Mercedes engine kept its sturdier but heavier successor, the D Va, barely able to hold its own against a new generation of Allied biplanes as 1918 dawned.

By mid-1917 even Gustave Delage had read the handwriting on the wall and was trying out a two-spar lower wing on a Nieuport 24. In November the Nieuport 28, a true biplane with a 160hp Gnome rotary engine, completed its first test flights. In spite of its 123mph speed and sprightly handling characteristics, the Nieuport 28 was too late to break the grip that the hardy SPAD VII and XIII biplanes had established in the *escadrilles de chasse*. It did, however, get a few months of frontline glory in American aero squadrons until enough SPAD XIIIs became available to take its place.

Like Nieuport, Albatros paid a price for overcommitment to the sesquiplane formula. In early 1918 it was ordered to license produce a biplane design from the very rival it had displaced more than a year earlier – the Fokker D VII. And while that superb original design regained Germany a measure of primacy over the Western Front, Anthony Fokker came around full circle by adapting its box spar cantilever wing structure to his first monoplane fighter since 1916 – the E V, later redesignated D VIII.

OPPOSITE TOP

Replicas of the old adversaries can be seen in California's San Diego Air and Space Museum. Here, a Fokker E III bearing the serial of the aeroplane in which Oblt Max Immelmann died on 18 June 1916 is displayed beneath a Nieuport 11 marked as Sgt G. Raoul Lufbery's N1256 of N124. (Jon Guttman)

OPPOSITE BOTTOM

A replica Fokker E V in *Jasta* 6 markings from August 1918 at Kermit Weeks' Fantasy of Flight museum in Polk City, Florida. Using Fokker's box spar cantilever structure, the E V revived the monoplane as a viable fighter, although circumstances prevented the aeroplane from living up to its potential. (Jon Guttman)

FURTHER READING

BOOKS

Brannon, D. Edgar, *Fokker Eindecker in Action* (Squadron/Signal Publications, Inc. Carrollton, Texas, 1996)

Cooksley, Peter, *Nieuport Fighters in Action*, (Squadron/Signal Publications, Inc., Carrollton, Texas, 1997)

DogFight No. 4 – Nieuport Contre Fokker (Janvier-Février, Aéro-Éditions International, Siret, France, 2007)

Franks, Norman, *Sharks Among Minnows* (Grub Street, London, 2001)

Franks, Norman and Bailey, Frank W., *Above the Lines* (Grub Street, London, 1993)

Franks, Norman, Bailey Frank W. and Duiven, Rick, *The Jasta War Chronology* (Grub Street, London, 1998)

Pieters, Walter, *The Belgian Air Service in the First World War* (Aeronaut Books, Indio, California, 2010)

Revell, Alex, *British Single-Seater Fighter Squadrons on the Western Front in World War I* (Schiffer Publishing Ltd., Atlgen, Pennsylvania, 2006)

Revell, Alex, *Victoria Cross – World War I Airmen and Their Aircraft*
(Flying Machines Press, Stratford, Connecticut, 1997)

Shores, Christopher, Franks, Norman and Guest, Russell, *Above the Trenches*
(Grub Street, London, 1990)

MAGAZINE ARTICLES

Grosz, Peter M., 'So, What's New About Stealth?' *Air International*, September
1986, pp.147–151

Jarrett, Philip, 'Fokker Five-O-Nine', *Cross & Cockade Great Britain Journal*, Vol. 12
No. 1, Spring 1981, pp.1–9

Puglisi, W. G., 'Letters from German *Jagdstaffel* Personnel of World War I', *Cross &
Cockade (USA) Journal*, Vol. 1, No. 1, Spring 1960, p. 39

INDEX